DEMOLITION WASTE

DEMOLITION WASTE

An examination of the arisings, end-uses and disposal of demolition wastes in Europe and the potential for further recovery of materials from these wastes

prepared for
THE COMMISSION OF THE EUROPEAN COMMUNITIES

by
ENVIRONMENTAL RESOURCES LIMITED

THE CONSTRUCTION PRESS
LANCASTER   LONDON   NEW YORK

The Construction Press Ltd,
Lancaster, England.

A subsidiary company of Longman Group Ltd, London.
Associated companies, branches and representatives
throughout the world.

Published in the United States of America by
Longman Inc, New York.

Published for
The Commission of the European
Communities, Directorate-General for
Scientific and Technical Information
and Information Management,
Luxembourg.

EUR 6619EN

First published 1980

British Library Cataloguing in Publication Data
Environmental Resources Limited
    Demolition waste.
    1. Construction industry – European Economic
    Community countries – Waste disposal
    2. Wrecking – Waste disposal
    3. Recycling (Waste, etc.) – European Economic
    Community countries
    I. Title   II. Commission of the European Communities
    624.1   TH153

ISBN 0-86095-865-5

Printed by: Pitman Press Limited, Bath, England.

Contents

List of tables

List of figures

Report summary

It is estimated that some 80 million tonnes of demolition wastes and a similar quantity of construction wastes arise in the EEC each year. The composition of demolition waste is approximately 57% by weight masonry, 37% concrete, and 2% timber. The remaining 4% comprises gypsum and plaster products, ferrous metals, and small amounts of non-ferrous metals, plastics, glass, asbestos products, and fittings and coverings of various kinds.

Arisings of demolition waste are expected to double by the year 2000, and triple by 2020. The composition is also expected to change substantially, with the proportion of concrete increasing to 80% by 2000.

The environmental impact attributable to these wastes is most apparent in the disturbance, noise and dust caused during on-site processing and transport of materials. Some recommendations are given by which this impact could be reduced, but reduction of on-site noise and disturbance cannot be significantly effected without a substantial increase in operational costs.

Because of their generally inert character, final disposal of these wastes presents problems only when the absence of suitable landfill sites causes substantial increase in transport costs.

Recovery of materials is almost wholly restricted to uncontaminated "high value" products, notably ferrous and non-ferrous metals and some timber. The main obstacles to further recovery include the fragmented organisational structure of the industry, unsteady local demand, lack of disseminated information and the frequent use of time penalty clauses in demolition contracts.

The materials which offer the greatest potential for further recovery are mixed demolition rubble, uncontaminated concrete wastes, timber and steel. The report examines the possibility of centralised large-scale rubble processing plant and concludes that such plant could well be economic particularly when there is no nearby source of natural aggregate material.

Definitions of terms established by CEC

Waste : Any substance or object which the holder disposes of or is required to dispose of pursuant to the provisions of national law in force

Disposal* : (a) The collection, sorting, transport and treatment of waste as well as its storage and tipping above or under ground, and

(b) the transformation operations necessary for its re-use, recovery or recycling

This disposal, other than destruction, would lead to one or more of the following phases: reclamation, recycling, re-use and/or by-product generation

Reclamation : The separation out of the material or products from waste, ie, all methods allowing the recovery and use of material from waste: recycling, re-use and the generation of by-products

Recycling : The reclamation and subsequent use of a material for the manufacture and/or fabrication of that same or similar product from which the waste originated (eg, use of cullet to manufacture bottles)

Re-use : The reclamation of a product in its end-use form and its subsequent use in this same form (eg, use of glass as bottles)

By-product generation (regeneration) : The reclamation and subsequent use of a material and/or fabrication of a product different from that from which the material was reclaimed (eg, use of cullet for road making)

End-use : The final use to which a material is put after which it has no further value other than in the secondary-materials' market

* In this report, the use of the word 'disposal' is mostly used in the context of 'final disposal', ie, as an alternative to reclamation, recovery, recycling, etc, as defined above.

Abbreviations

ANCE	:	Associazione Nazionale Constuttori Edili
BABEX	:	Association of Dutch Demolition Contractors Licensed to Use Explosives
BRE	:	Building Research Establishment
CEI	:	Council for Engineering Institutions
CEP	:	Conseils Économiques Provincial
CRESME	:	Centro Ricerche Economiche Sociologiche di Mercato nell'Edilizia
CSTB	:	Centre Scientifique et Technique du Bâtiment
CSTC	:	Centre Scientifique et Technique de la Construction
CTB	:	Centre Technique de Bois
CUR	:	Stiching Commissie voor Uitvoering van Research
DDIR	:	Demolition and Dismantling Industry Register
DIN	:	Deutsche Industrie-Norm
DOE	:	Department of the Environment
EDA	:	European Demolition Association
EIB	:	Economische Instituut voor de Bouwbedrijven
FED	:	Fédération des Entrepreneurs de Demolition
HMSO	:	Her Majesty's Stationery Office
IDA	:	Industrial Development Authority
IRRS	:	Institute for Industrial Research and Standards
NFDC	:	National Federation of Demolition Contractors
OECD	:	Organisation for Economic Co-operation and Development
RILEM	:	Réunion Internationale des Laboratoires d'Essais et de Récherches sur les Matériaux et les Constructions
SVA	:	Stickting Verwijdering Afvalstoffen
TNO	:	Organisatie voor Toegepast Natuurwetenschappelijk Onderzoek
TRRL	:	Transport and Road Research Laboratory

1. Introduction

1.1   Objectives

The objectives of this study on demolition wastes are as follows:

-     estimate the quantities of demolition and related wastes arising in the EEC and assess the different types;

-     examine the current uses for materials/products recovered from these wastes, and estimate the present extent of recovery in member states, and review current and new means of waste handling and recovery;

-     examine the economics of handling, recovering and disposing of these wastes;

-     identify the scope for additional waste recovery, and the obstacles to achieving further re-use of materials, suggesting how these obstacles might be overcome;

-     discuss the environmental implications of recovery of demolition wastes;

-     make recommendations to the Commission on action that might be taken.

1.2   Organisation of the report

The report is structured into seven separate sections:-

1.   Introduction.
2.   Composition and Sources of wastes.
3.   Quantity of wastes arising.
4.   Economics.
5.   Potential for further reclamation.
6.   Environmental considerations.
7.   Conclusions and recommendations.

Much of the data obtained during the course of the study has been removed to the Appendices of the report, including specialist information on detailed issues such as asbestos arisings in demolition waste. Also described in the Appendices are reviews of current research, public authorities and research organisations, and national regulations pertaining to demolition and the reclamation and disposal of wastes.

1.3   Data

Information for the study was collected primarily from detailed interviews held with public and private authorities and organisations in each of the member states. These data were augmented by whatever information was available in the literature.

The interviews were designed to provide information on:

-        The demolition industry: its structure, pertinent regulations, research, trends in housing stock and demolition, methods of demolition, etc.

-        Materials: quantities and types of wastes generated, composition of structures, new materials usage and corresponding future trends of demolition wastes.

-        Reclamation: material quantities, purchasers and difficulties associated with reclamation of particular wastes. Research and potential for further reclamation.

-        Transport and handling: waste separation techniques, transport network and costs, disposal methods and charges, environmental considerations.

Amongst the organisations contacted were:

-        the central government agencies of the Community member nations;

-        local authorities;

-        international organisations with an interest in demolition waste arisings (e.g. European Demolition Association in The Hague);

-        national research institutes and universities;

-        national trade organisations and individual demolition contractors;

-        other organisations with an interest in the handling, reclamation or disposal of demolition wastes.

There is one point that we wish to stress. There is a shortage of reliable quantitative information many of the areas covered by this report. In particular, there is a deficit of data in two main areas:-

2

i.   quantity of demolition wastes;

ii.   composition of demolition wastes.

It has therefore been necessary either to quote data that we have been unable to verify or to develop estimates from what information that is available. The estimates given in Section 3 therefore provide _initial_ indications of the quantities and compositions of materials involved, and as further information becomes available, they should be verified. We therefore caution that the figures quoted in this report should be used only in this context.

1.4   Terminology

We have attempted to make some distinction between **types** of demolition waste that are generated in the Community. Terms such as 'demolition wastes', 'construction wastes', 'builders rubble' etc. are often used without either the source or nature of waste being clearly defined. For the purpose of this report, we have divided demolition and related wastes into two basic types:

-       Demolition waste: this represents material that arises as a direct result of the demolition of buildings and structures.

-       Construction waste: this represents wastes generated by the following materials;

        i.   earthworks arising from the excavation of land;

        ii.   off-cuts, excess and broken materials arising from new construction work;

        iii.   materials arising from the repair and maintenance of buildings, roads and waterways;

        iv.   materials arising from the rehabilitation of housing or reconstruction of non-residential buildings.

Furthermore, in our estimates of quantities of waste materials, we have distinguished between total materials that arise through demolition or construction activity in the Community, and waste materials that present problems of disposal.

1.5   Acknowledgements

Environmental Resources Limited would like to express their gratitude for the considerable assistance they have received from governments, local authorities and industry in all the member countries of the Community during the preparation of this report.

2. Demolition and the nature of wastes

2.1 Introduction

In this section we have identified the types of material that are generated by demolition or construction activities, their sources, methods of handling and current recovery and disposal practice.

2.2 Principal sources and types of materials

In Table 2.2(a) we identify the principal types of demolition and construction waste and their sources, and indicate those materials which are normally considered for recovery.

2.2.1 Wastes arising from residential demolition

In most member states the rate of housing demolition has declined since the late 1960's. Two main factors are responsible for this decline:

- The requirement for housing demolition is often directly linked to the rate of new residential construction, which has itself declined due to the general decrease in economic activity in Western Europe over the past few years.

- There has been a tendency over the past ten years to rehabilitate housing, rather than to demolish and construct new housing.

The residential buildings that have been demolished in this decade, and those that are currently being taken down, mostly comprise the more elderly housing stock which is by current standards dangerous or inadequate. Many such dwellings are de-molished by virtue of various "slum clearance" policies, and were built during the latter half of the nineteenth century, or in the early years of the twentieth century. The materials of construction of such dwellings were similar in all member states - usually comprising load-bearing brick or stone walls with an inner covering of plaster, often with timber framework, and with slate roofing tiles.

Table 2.2(a)

PRINCIPAL SOURCES AND TYPES OF MATERIALS

Type of waste	Principal Sources	Materials which are normally recovered
Demolition (Masonry, plain and reinforced concrete, ferrous and non-ferrous metals, timber, tiles, plastics, glass, gypsum and plaster products, fittings.)	Residential and non-residential buildings. Civil engineering structures (bridges, chimney-stacks etc.)	Metals for recycling. Some rubble for fill. Some fittings for re-sale. Some timber for re-use. Small quantity of bricks.
Construction (Mostly earth and stones, some broken bricks and tiles, excess concrete, timber off-cuts etc.)	Excavation of land; off-cuts and broken materials from new construction work.	Earthworks for fill.
Repair and Maintenance As for demolition waste. Concrete, masonry, earthworks, bituminous products.	Reconstruction of buildings. Maintenance of transport systems.	As for demolition waste. Rubble for fill.

Demolition of more modern housing occurs mainly to facilitate new development - roads, motorways, new housing or industrial development. Other causes, such as construction faults (e.g. high alumina cement in multi-storey appartment buildings) add to the number of such buildings demolished each year in the Community, but their significance is small compared with the wastes that are generated by the more elderly housing stock.

2.2.2   Wastes arising from non-residential demolition

The major classifications of these types of buildings are as commercial (shops and offices) and as industrial (factories and workshops). There is however a third group of buildings which do not obviously lie in either of these categories, such as churches, schools, hospitals, hotels, amusement centres and the like.

Details of the numbers and types of non-residential buildings demolished are often not available for a particular country, and it is therefore difficult to estimate the quantity and quality of wastes arising from this sector.

However, some general observations may be made for buildings demolished in the non-residential sector. Very often, the useful life of industrial buildings is relatively short. A design lifetime of 10 - 20 years is not uncommon, although a more realistic average lifetime is believed to be nearer to 40 years. The demand for different types of commercial property can change drastically over a relatively short period of time, and offices or shops in a particular area may become redundant 20 or 30 years after their construction.

In general, it is reasonable to assume that the average lifetime of both industrial and commercial property is significantly less than that for housing. In our forecasts of future wastes arising, we have assumed an average lifetime of 40 years for the non-residential sector.

The kinds of materials that arise from this sector vary according to the type, and age of structure demolished. Industrial buildings, which are very often less than 40 years old, are almost all constructed in concrete and steel. Commercial buildings and hotels may be either concrete or masonry based; in the latter case, there will be significant quantities of iron and timber.

2.2.3   Wastes arising from the demolition of other structures

We include in this sector both civil engineering structures (airport runways, bridges, tunnels, chimney stacks etc.) and hydraulic engineering structures (water treatment plant, resevoirs, river works, harbours and docks).

Actual demolition of either of these types of structure does not often occur - such structures may often be repaired or improved, but complete demolition is rare.

Where demolition does take place however, significant contributions to waste arisings in a particular locality and at a particular time may occur. For civil engineering structures, the type and age of the structure tends to dictate the type of waste generated - for example, masonry, iron or steel, or reinforced concrete wastes may arise from the demolition of bridges, and the particular materials arising depend to a considerable extent upon their age.

National variations are of particular import where waste arisings from the demolition of hydraulic engineering structures are concerned. For maritime nations, demolition work at harbours and docks may be an influential factor, and for those nations that utilise inland waterways to a great extent (Belgium, France, the Netherlands and Germany), work aimed at improving or maintaining canals, including the demolition of redundant installations, can give rise to large quantities of waste materials. In such cases the resulting material, mostly concrete but possibly some masonry depending upon the age of the strucutre, is usually re-used on site as bulk-fill.

2.2.4   Wastes arising from construction activities

We have identified the following four major waste streams generated by construction activity:

-      Excavation wastes: these arise as a result of excavation of land for such diverse works as new construction, roads, canals, resevoirs and the like. A portion of the excavated material is always used on-site (e.g. cut-and-fill technique for road making, construction of embankments, surrounding hills, as fill for marshy and low-land areas, etc.). In many instances, the whole of this material may be used.

-      Construction wastes: when sheets, tiles or timber are being cut on site to design specifications, sizing wastes often arise as the design does not normally take into account the practical sizes of building materials. Furthermore, material quality as delivered may differ from that specified, or be inconsistent. This can lead to substantial rejection. Finally, mishandling of materials often results in significant quantities of breakages. The amount and type of wastes thus generated obviously depend upon the type of structure, and the control effected by the individual building or construction company. In general though, the major waste materials arising from this activity are timber off-cuts, excess concrete, and broken bricks, aggregate blocks and tiles.

-      Wastes arising from repair and maintenance: waste arisings from repair and maintenance of buildings are not believed to be significant. Although every building will have substantial expenditure in terms of repair and maintenance during its life-span, there will be little structural alteration associated with this type of work, and the waste arisings will therefore be small.

However, repair and maintenance of other construction works do give rise to substantial quantities of wastes. In particular, maintenance of transport systems (roads and canals) can give rise to large quantities of asphalt, soil, rock and concrete. Road repair is a significant item of expenditure in every member state. Maintenance and improvement of the inland waterway system however is most significant in Germany, the Netherlands, Belgium and France.

–   Waste arising from reconstruction and rehabilitation:
rehabilitation of housing usually entails the complete
stripping-out of the interior of the dwelling, leaving
only structural inner walls, New partition walls will
be constructed, the electrical circuit replaced, and new
fittings installed. In many cases, the roofing tiles
might be partially, or wholly replaced, and timbers
renewed where necessary.

The main waste materials from the rehabilitation of
housing will thus be gypsum products and plasterboard,
timber, broken tiles and diverse materials such as
porcelain kitchen, bathroom and sanitary equipment,
floor coverings, wallpaper, etc.

Non-residential buildings often change their ownership,
or their use, several times during their life-span. A
new owner may require different apportionment of the
available area – a new use will invariably require this.
Partial reconstruction thus becomes necessary.

Very often, the whole interior of the building, with the
exception of structural walls and members,will be removed.
The types of wastes thus produced will include masonry
and concrete, steel, gypsum products, plasterboard and
timber.

2.3 Handling and transport considerations

2.3.1 The movement of materials

The simplified model shown in Figure 2.3(a) illustrates the
movement of waste materials generated by construction or
demolition activities.

We discuss below the four main types of activity engaged in by
the demolition contractor which are affected by handling and/or
transport considerations.

2.3.2 Recovery prior to demolition

Waste material from demolition or construction is normally
sorted at the site into salvageable, and non-salvageable
fractions.

The extent to which recovery is carried out is influenced:

–   by the time available for the job (in particular whether
or not there is a penalty clause)

–   by the attitude of the contractor, and whether or not
he sees recovery as a major source of income.

Most contractors will recover materials that are easily
accessible and which can be sold profitably (mainly ferrous and
non-ferrous metals).

Figure 2.3(a)   MOVEMENT OF CONSTRUCTION AND DEMOLITION WASTES

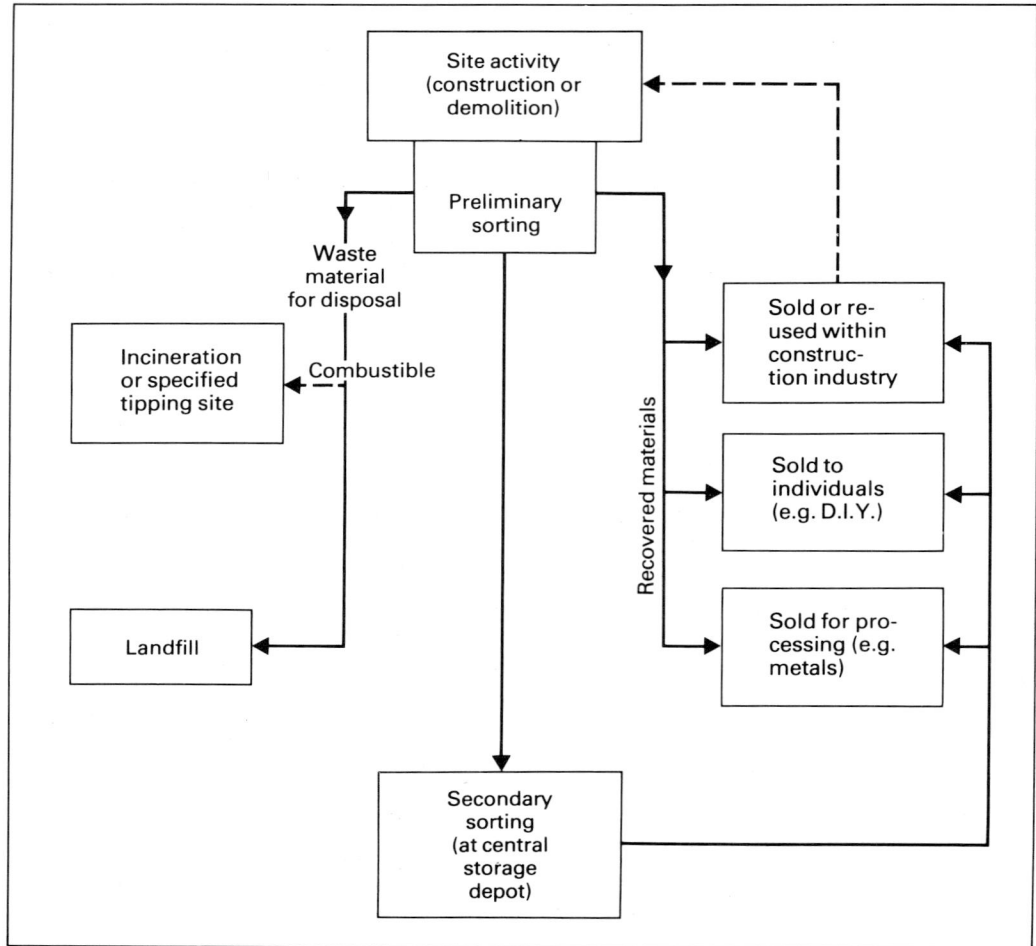

It is normal practice for the contractor to send a team of men
into the building prior to demolition in order to remove all
accessible metals (piping, conduits, wrought-iron staircases,
radiators, brass fittings, etc.), re-saleable or usable timbers
(doors, good quality window-frames, floorboards), diverse
fittings (cupboards, baths, sink units, shelving, roofing tiles
and roofing timbers.

If there is a large quantity of good quality timber available
from such operations, a timber merchant specialising in second-
hand woodwork may be contacted, and will purchase most of the
wood ex-site. Some timbers may be retained by the contractor
for use on-site (i.e. for shoring purposes, or for fence work).
Various fittings may also be sold ex-site to small second-hand
merchants.

2.3.3   Demolition techniques

After the interior of a building has been stripped out, the
actual demolition of the building will take place. The
method used will depend upon the type and size of the structure,
its materials of construction, its location, and upon the
requirement for materials reclamation.

Where possible, the structure will be demolished using a tracked vehicle to push or pull the structure down. In many situations however this may not be done - the structure might be too strong or, as is very often the case, it might be situated in a confined space (e.g. an inner-city area). In such cases other demolition methods will be employed:-

- Where reinforced concrete structures are to be demolished, a favourite technique is the use of a crane and demo- lition ball. The controlled swing of the ball breaks the concrete away to expose some of the reinforcing, which can then be cut up into manageable lengths using oxyacetylene torches. This method is also suitable for the demolition of large areas of housing in a city (e.g. slum clearance). However, the ball-and-crane may only be used in relatively isolated areas where there is no danger from flying debris.

- In inner-city areas, where there is no room for large mechanical equipment to operate, buildings are most often demolished by hand. The equipment that may be used ranges from sledge-hammers and crow-bars to hand-held pneumatic drills. The general method of procedure conforms to the general rule that demolition proceeds in the reverse order of construction.

- Explosives are used in particular instances (e.g. the deliberate collapse of masonry or reinforced concrete chimneys). Obviously, this method can only be used in isolated areas. Another limiting factor is that the instantaneous demolition of a large and heavy mass will produce considerable vibration and shock-waves which could affect nearby buildings, underground pipework (e.g. gas mains) and tunnels (e.g. road-tunnels, under- ground rail network). The use of explosives must therefore be carefully controlled.

Influence on recovery. Obviously the type of demolition technique utilised will affect the possibility for further recovery of materials. Hand demolition will enable sorting of materials as they are encountered. At the other end of the scale, explosives demolition will fracture most of the component materials of the structure, and will ensure that they are mixed together.

If it is intended to salvage the brickwork, the use of a tracked vehicle fitted with a "pusher arm" or "back-actor" will enable the wall to be pushed, or pulled to the ground. As the wall impacts against the ground , the bricks separate from their mortar with very little breakage.

Storage of reclaimed materials. At secure demolition sites, salvaged materials which have not been sold directly from the site will be retained there until the work is complete. More often, however, the materials are transported to a central storage area.

All demolition companies of a significant size (i.e. excluding the 2-3 man "casual" firms) will have some form of central storage area. In many cases, this might only be a corner of a yard set aside for the collection of metals and valuable fittings. Larger companies may have considerable storage facilities, at which full-time staff may be employed to sort and sell salvaged materials, In most cases, however, metals are brought to such an area to be weighed, and kept there until a sufficient quantity has accumulated so that transport costs may be minimised. They are then delivered to a specialist metals dealer and sold.

2.3.4   Disposal practise

Once the building or structure has been demolished, and all reclamable materials either sold ex-site, or taken to some central storage depot for later re-sale, the resulting rubble has to be disposed of. In general, this is removed by road to the nearest tipping site.

The view of controlled landfill site operators differ on the disposal of demolition rubble:

-       If the rubble is relatively contaminant-free (i.e. free of degradable/combustible material such as wood) and is relatively small-sized (i.e. no large masses of plain or reinforced concrete), many authorities actively seek the rubble to use as cover material between layers of domestic wastes. In such cases the requirement for the material is reflected in the charges for tipping, i.e. they may be nominal charges or even zero-rated.

-       Other landfill operators who have adequate supplies of earth and top-soil for covering material will not require this type of rubble, and may charge the same rate for its disposal as is charged for domestic or other industrial wastes.

Excavation wastes, which constitute the bulk of construction wastes, do not normally present disposal problems, as this material is often required as fill or cover material at nearby construction sites. This material may be taken to licensed tipping areas, but normally only when the tipping charges for this kind of material are non-existent, or negligible.

Disposal problems. Construction and demolition waste tends to be viewed as a disposal problem only when it is heavily contaminated with timber, plastics, metals or large pieces of concrete.

Wastes containing large quantities of timber can pose particular problems. Many tip operators will refuse to accept such wastes. In these cases incineration is a solution. However, incineration charges are substantially greater than tipping charges (see Section 4.2.5) and where possible contractors will seek alternative means of disposal (e.g. burning on site).

12

In Germany, demolition and construction rubble is required by law to be taken to specific tipping sites, which may be publicly or privately owned (1). In the Netherlands (2) specific sites are made available which accept only inert industrial wastes, although there is as yet no legislation to prevent uncontrolled tipping.

2.3.5   Transport systems

Road Transport. Road transport accounts for almost all of the movement of demolition and construction wastes in the European Community. We encountered two demolition contractors (one in the U.K. and one in the Netherlands) who had used the inland waterway network in the past, but both claimed that this was no longer economic.

Transport of materials to tipping areas may be undertaken by the contractor or by transport companies. In the mid-1960's when there was a great deal of demolition work available, many of the larger companies built up their transport fleet, and a significant proportion of the waste was carried by contractor-owned vehicles. This situation is now changed and transport companies carry the majority of materials.

Problems associated with transport. One particular problem that has become apparent in recent years due to the change-over to contracted-out transport is the problem of illegal tipping. The demolition contractor will tend to accept the lowest quote for the disposal of waste ex-site. An owner-driver, seeking work, can then sometimes under-cut the price offered by a reputable transport company by tipping the wastes on a nearby construction site, or some other empty area. It is extremely difficult to prevent this happening. In Nice, the charges for tipping construction wastes at public sites are deliberately kept low in order to prevent such indiscriminate tipping, even though it is estimated that the costs of disposal (site management and ownership, compacting charges, etc.) are at least ten times the amount charged.

Other transport systems. Wastes are occasionally transported via a transfer station. To the best of our knowledge, those transfer stations which will accept certain quantities of demolition and construction wastes, are operated primarily to handle domestic refuse. (An exception exists in Berlin, where large quantities of demolition wastes are transferred to barges for transport to the German Democratic Republic). Most waste transfer stations in the E.E.C. transfer waste by road, though a few operate with rail or barge (e.g. London, Berlin). Transfer of wastes involves an additional stage of handling, and therefore additional costs, which must be more than compensated for by savings in overall transport costs. In the case of most demolition and construction wastes, possible savings for the contractor in transport costs through transfer by road are only likely to occur where the amounts of waste involved are small (loads of a few tonnes only). The payload limits on the transfer vehicles are similar to those for the larger vehicles used for hauling demolition wastes from sites so that, for larger loads of waste, haulage direct from site of origin to disposal site will be a cheaper option for the contractor. The potential for transport cost savings through transfer by rail or barge is greater due to the very large payloads that can be carried in this way, but the circumstances in the Community where this option is available to a contractor are rare. Undoubtedly, direct transport by road will continue to be the only means available for the vast majority of building and demolition wastes in the E.E.C.

2.4   Existing uses for materials and the extent of recovery

2.4.1   Uses for recovered materials

Existing products and materials that may be recovered from demolition or construction wastes are:

-        materials for recycling; i.e. for use as feedstock (raw materials) in production of the same or similar products (essentially only applies to metals)

-        items for re-use; including structural steel components, bricks, stone blocks, roofing slates, and sometimes good timber, fittings, electric motors etc.

-        materials for use in lower grade applications (mainly mineral materials for hardcore and for fill applications).

There is little variation within the Community between the recovery practises of individual demolition contractors, but recovery of particular materials is dependant on local influences (e.g. urban or rural location, transport distances, tipping charges etc.)

Materials for recyling. The only materials recovered during demolition activity for recyling are ferrous and non-ferrous metals. These are sold at normal scrap metal rates to specialist metal merchants.

Items for re-use. Some structural steelwork reclaimed by the demolition contractor may be sold for re-use. This applies principally to rolled-steel joists. Good quality timbers are often removed prior to demolition - doors, window-frames and panelling for re-sale, together with floorboards and structural timbers for use within the construction industry (as hoarding, fences and for shoring). In some areas bricks, stonework and roofing tiles are also salvaged for re-sale because of the high local demand.

Materials for re-use in lower grade applications. After demolition the resulting debris constitutes a heterogenous mass of rubble, and costs of separation are normally such as to exclude further recovery of individual materials. A portion of the rubble is used in all of the Member States as bulk-fill material, usually for the construction of embankments (alongside canals or roads), or for landscaping purposes. Another popular use is as temporary road surface material at construction and landfill sites.

2.4.2   The extent of recovery

Metals. There is a good and consistent market for all of the non-ferrous metals (mainly copper, lead, zinc and aluminium) arising from demolition in the Community. In the view of all demolition contractors interviewed, non-ferrous metals recovery can be practically considered as approaching 100%.

Similarly, all easily accessible ferrous metals are salvaged. There is however a significant proportion of ferrous material that is not presently reclaimed. This comprises much of the steel in reinforced concrete, where the costs of separating the bound steel from the concrete often outweigh the value of the reclaimed material.

Timber. It is difficult to classify specific national or regional areas in which timber reclamation is particularly high, due to the influences exercised by individuals.

In rural areas, timber wastes from demolition and off-cuts from construction are often sold to farmers for use in construction and maintenance of agricultural buildings and structures (barns, sheds, fencing, etc.).

In large urban connurbations, major demolition contractors often have storage depots to which good quality timbers are taken for later sale. There is also high demand in these areas from the construction industry and from DIY individuals, but constraints caused by the presence of time-penalty clauses in demolition contracts often adversely affect timber reclamation.

The total quantity of timber reclaimed is not therefore particularly high. Estimates from contractors suggest that probably less than 20% of the total wood wastes from demolition handled in the Community will be re-used, and that this figure can vary according to individual practice from 0% - 50%

Other items for re-use. Recovery of such items as bricks and roofing tiles is highly location-specific. Very small markets exist in most countries for particular types of brickwork for historic or aesthetic reasons (e.g. 14th and 15th century hand-made bricks in Copenhagen) but generally speaking masonry is regarded as part of the waste stream.

In certain parts of the U.K. there is a high demand for clean bricks in good condition. This demand is caused by the desire of local authorities to retain the original character of particular areas. One local authority in the London area has for four years attempted to use second-hand facing bricks in all new housing schemes in order to blend the new housing into its environment. This authority currently has problems in obtaining sufficient supplies for its needs but it was emphasised that where possible they would use second-hand bricks in preference to new ones.

In the U.K. and in Denmark, there are significant markets for the older type red-clay roofing tiles, for use in repair and maintenance and occasionally in new construction.

15

However, in terms of the Community's demolition waste stream, the degree of recovery and re-use of such products is small.

Rubble. The amount of rubble that is used in the Community for such secondary purposes as bulk-fill, surface material and the like depends greatly upon weather conditions. In a wet season, when there is a very high demand for temporary road surfaces (at construction sites, landfill sites etc.), up to 50% of the Community's arisings of demolition rubble may be accounted for. Throughout the year however, we estimate that between 20 - 25% of demolition rubble is used for such secondary uses.

Wastes for road-making operations. Wastes from the construction, or reconstruction of roads and pavements can be generated in significant quantities. Road reconstruction in particular often gives rise to large quantities of broken concrete and bituminous concrete wastes. There is however virtually no re-use of these materials in new road contruction, although some research is being undertaken in this field (3).

Other materials. Other materials which can arise from the demolition of structures or from construction activity include gypsum and plasterboard, asbestos and asbestos-cement products, ceramic sanitary ware and other fittings, glass, bitumen and bituminous products, plastic piping and other plastic products. All of these materials arise only in very small quantities and, with the exception of household and other fittings, are not presently recovered. Fittings of good quality and modern design can often be sold either directly by the contractor to individuals, or to specialist secondhand merchants.

2.4.3   Problems associated with recovery

Time penalty clauses. The major problem affecting salvage of materials from demolition is the influence of time penalty clauses in demolition contracts. At best, salvage of low value materials and products such as timber, unbroken bricks and roofing tiles, fittings etc. is a low profit exercise (due to handling, sorting, transport and storage costs) and no contractor will increase salvage of these materials at the expense of exceeding the allocated time for the contract.

Contamination. The second influence which tends to inhibit recovery is contamination. Certain potentially recoverable materials are not reclaimed because they are highly contaminated by other low value materials. Copper present in electric wiring is not recovered because of the expense of separating it from its insulation. Other small quantities of non-ferrous metals are not reclaimed because of separation costs - e.g. lead pipes which are buried in the ground. The two most significant materials for which contamination problems tend to inhibit reclamation are steel reinforcing bound in concrete, and demolition rubble.

a.   Reinforced concrete: separation of bound steel from reinforced concrete is highly energy intensive. A wrecking-ball is normally used, but with mesh reinforcing, the concrete may only crack and in some cases will then adhere even more tightly to its reinforcing. There is

currently very little reclamation of steel, or recovery
of concrete from such structures. There is however
considerable potential for recovery of both of these
materials and this is discussed later in Section 5.

b.   Demolition rubble: this comprises a mixture of broken
        brick or stonework and plain or reinforced concrete.
        Other materials such as slate, gypsum and plaster
        products, timber, glass, plastics, etc. are also
        present in relatively small concentrations. It is the
        presence of such contaminants in the rubble that tends
        to prevent its use in end-uses other than bulk-fill
        and cover material.

        A recent OECD report (4) concluded that providing steel
        and other deleterious material is removed from demo-
        lition rubble, brick and concrete wastes, old bitumous
        concrete pavements and old Portland cement concrete
        pavements can be re-used in road construction with excel-
        lent results. The potential is as yet largely undeveloped,
        but significant savings in quantities of both aggregates
        and binding materials can be expected.

        A private company in the South East of England processes
        demolition rubble to a form in which it can be used in
        place of natural aggregates for road building (5). The
        company accepts and sometimes pays a small amount for
        clean rubble from demolition contractors in the London
        area. Loads containing timber, unfired clay, reinforced
        concrete or significant quantities of other contaminants
        are not accepted. The rubble is size-reduced in a jaw
        crusher, screened at 90mm, and both the oversize and the
        undersize are sold. User experience indicates that the
        material is a good substitute for natural aggregates for
        both bulk-fill and sub-base use in road construction.

        There is considerable potential for increased use of
        demolition rubble as a substitute for natural aggregates,
        and this is discussed in greater depth in Section 5.

2.5   The structure of the demolition industry

2.5.1   The demolition industry in the EEC is structured on a national
           basis. The majority of individual companies are small and employ
           only a handful of employees. Such companies normally undertake
           work only in their own localities or regions.

           However, changes are beginning to become evident in the industrial
           structure, caused principally by the increasing complexity of
           demolition work, and the need for expensive capital equipment.

           In particular, two influences have favoured the development of
           either relatively large companies who must be prepared to travel
           to other areas of the Community when work in their own region is
           short, or small specialist companies who by nature of their
           specialisation seek work throughout the Community.

- the increasing requirement for <u>professional expertise</u> has tended to cause small specialist companies to expand, or to merge with companies of other specialities. A small general demolition contractor is often neither capable nor sufficiently equipped to demolish large structures containing re-inforced, post-stressed or pre-tensioned concrete;

- the increasing requirement for <u>environmental protection</u> and <u>safety at work</u> in the Community has favoured larger companies who are better able to finance training of workers, and to bear the costs of equipment for reducing environmental nuisance (water-sprays for dust prevention, exhaust silencers on pneumatic plant, hoardings for protection from flying debris, etc.);

Both of these influences relate to <u>economies of scale</u>: up to a certain size, a large company is better able to withstand lean times, and take advantage of times of plenty. The larger company can also reduce costs by owning his own transport fleet and demolition/excavation machinery, and as often happens, leasing vehicles and machinery to other companies when they are not required. Furthermore, the larger company often has storage areas available, where saleable items can be held until market fluctuations maximise resale value.

2.5.2   <u>Major trade organisations</u>

The above factors have been recognised by demolition contractors in certain of the Member States of the Community for several years. In the Federal Republic of Germany, the Netherlands and the United Kingdom, strong associations of demolition contractors have emerged whose principal objectives are :

- to increase the professionalism of the industry (by training of employees, exchange of information, publications etc.);

- to represent the industry at national level, and act as the industry's spokesman;

- to improve and promote the image of the industry.

The three major trade organisations of these countries (Deutscher Abbruchverbrand (FRG), BABEX (Nl) and the National Federation of Demolition Contractors in the U.K.) collaborated together in 1976 in forming the <u>European Demolition Association</u> (EDA).

Among the objectives of the EDA is the achievement, at European level, of uniform working methods, safety regulations and also an exchange of experience. In addition, the EDA has developed contacts with the North American demolition industry, and has become involved with European research projects relating to demolition and the re-use of materials.

In other Community states, the demolition industry is not so well organised.

In France the industry is represented at local and national level by the Fédération des Entrepreneurs de Démolition (FED). The FED represents about 5% of all companies undertaking demolition work in France, but this 5% comprises demolition specialists who between them account for about 50% of total demolition work. At an international level, the Federation has been invited to join the European Demolition Association, but it is unlikely that the French demolition industry will take up membership until the industry itself is more stable and better organised nationally.

In Italy there is no organisation of demolition contractors, and there are therefore no national links with other demolition industry workers. However, the National Association of Construction Industries (ANCE) has recently held discussions with the EDA with a view to establishing a national demolition federation and associating with the European Association.

In Belgium major civil engineering demolition is sometimes undertaken by the Military, whilst the demolition of housing and other structures is carried out by a large number of very small companies, each employing only a handful of personnel. There is as yet no organisation of demolition contractors, although the Belgian Federation of Building Contractors (Belgische Landsbond der Bouwbedrijven en Openbare Werken) is currently attempting to organise demolition contractors within their federation.

In Ireland and in Luxembourg, the extent of demolition activity is so small that there is no requirement for a national association or federation. Demolition contractors in these countries invariably undertake other works (excavation and site-levelling, earth-moving and land-reclamation, plant-hire etc.),the demolition work itself being in many cases only a subsidiary portion of a companies normal work.

2.5.3   Other private organisations and interested bodies

The requirement for increased expertise and professionalism has resulted in a register of approved demolition companies in certain countries. In France, contractors may obtain professional standing from the "Organisme Professionnel de Qualification et de Classification du Bâtiment " (OPQCB). Upon application, and after suitable examination it may award "La Qualification des Entreprises du Bâtiment" to a particular company. This professional qualification may be given for different specialities and a "Specialité de Demolition" is included. Demolition companies who meet with given standards - namely safety standards and codes of pracrice - may thus become members of the professional register.

In the United Kingdom, the Demolition and Dismantling Industry Register (DDIR), which was set up jointly by the NFDC, trade unions, Federation of Scrap Dealers and the Department of the Environment, is the recognised register of competent firms, and due to a Department of the Environment recommendation of 1975, local authorities will normally only offer demolition, or dis-

mantling contracts to DDIR members. In addition, the NFDC has
recently established the "Institute of Demolition Engineers",
membership of which is reserved solely for those who have
satisfied the examining board of their professionalism. This
Institute is not, as yet, recognised by the Council for Engineering
Institutions (CEI).

Waste exchanges, to introduce potential purchasers of "waste"
material to the producers, have been set up in some countries
(e.g. the "Bulletin" of the U.K. Waste Materials Exchange and
the "Bourse des Dechets Industriels" recently created by the
Chambers of Commerce and Industry in Paris and in the Ile-de-
France). Although these exchanges are principally for chemical
and other industrial wastes, some components of demolition waste
(timber, crushed brick or concrete and metals may be included).

The scrap-metals industry acts in all countries in close co-
operation with the demolition industry. As mentioned earlier,
the Federation of Scrap Dealers in the United Kingdom co-
operated in establishing the DDIR, and in the Federal Republic
of Germany many demolition contractors are also members of the
Deutschen Schrottwirtschaft (German Scrap Federation).

3. Quantitative estimates of arisings of demolition and construction wastes

3.1   Introduction

3.1.1   Problems

There are a number of problems associated with preparing estimates of demolition and construction wastes:

-       Wastes arising from demolition or construction in the Community have not attracted as much attention from government and industry as have other categories of waste so statistical data on this subject are scarce and those that do exist tend to be of a broad, aggregated nature based on very limited sampling and actual measurement.

-       Definition and distinction of types of wastes: for instance, terms such as 'demolition wastes', 'construction wastes', 'excavation wastes', etc., are used often without being clearly defined.

-       The considerable variations in demolition and construction activity which occur from year to year; while structures are sometimes demolished and replaced due to structural obsolescence (e.g. safety hazards, fire damage, etc.), the greater part of demolition activity stems from the economic obsolescence of structures.

        In general there is a correlation between the level of demolition and construction activity and the level of activity in the economy generally. Research in the United States (42) has tended to support this view. The resulting short-term fluctuations in arisings of demolition and construction wastes are significant nationally and can be very important when estimating regional arisings. For example, the existence of a major urban renewal pro- gramme in a region will have a substantial impact on the amounts of waste generated during the life of the project.

3.1.2   Sources of waste

For the purposes of this study, we have focussed attention principally on those wastes associated with the demolition of existing
structures, while quantitative information on wastes from renovation
and new construction activity has been included whenever available.

It should be noted that construction wastes may often be readily
used as bulk fill, for landscaping, etc., and in the majority of
cases a high proportion of this material can eventually be accom-
modated on, or very near to, the site or origin. Care is therefore needed in estimating the quantities of these wastes arising,
particularly in the case of material from site preparation and
excavation, where a high proportion of the material generated does
not arise as a 'waste' in the sense that problems of transport and
disposal are thereby created.

3.2   Approaches to estimating arisings from demolition and construction
wastes

Bearing in mind the serious problems involved in trying to estimate
current arisings of demolition wastes mentioned above, there are
in essence two basic approaches that may be adopted for this purpose, and which may be broadly described as the 'input' approach
and the 'output' approach.

3.2.1   The 'input' approach

This method relies on analysing the materials that originally
went into the construction of structures being demolished today,
and requires at least the following information to be available
as inputs for the calculation:

i.   the quantities of various materials that have gone into
          different kinds of structures presently standing; that
          is, potential candidates for demolition;

ii.   the total number of structures represented by these
          quantities of materials;

iii.   the characteristics of structures which have recently
          been, or will shortly be, demolished, in particular the
          function of buildings (industrial, commercial, residential),
          type of construction, and the distribution of ages of
          structures at demolition.

While information of this degree of detail may well be available
for certain areas or cities within the Community, it is certainly
not available for the entire Community. This is especially so in
respect of information on i. and ii. for, in order to attain
even a moderately reliable estimate on an input basis of current
arisings of demolition wastes, it would be necessary to have data
on the consumption of building materials in each Member State for
each year since before the end of the last century. Even if
sufficient data were available, the method itself incorporates
substantial scope for error, for example:

- structures being demolished today will often have been modified and/or extended sometime during their lifetimes, which will affect the quantities and types of material generated at demolition;

- the set of buildings being demolished does not generally constitute a homogeneous combination of all types and sizes of structures, so the actual content of structures presently being demolished may not be the same as that based on the calculated content of an average building;

- a significant amount of demolition material remains on the site as backfill and levelling material, and the foundations are frequently left intact; adjusting for such 'losses' would be extremely difficult.

3.2.2   The 'output' approach

Estimating demolition or construction waste arisings on an output basis involves trying to determine the quantity of wastes actually being produced. This may take the form of identifying the structures demolished (or erected, in the case of construction wastes) over a period of time and sampling of the quantities and types of material that arise from each class of structure, or, more commonly, recording and sampling the demolition material (or construction waste) actually being removed and disposed of. Many national estimates of current arisings rely primarily on an 'output' approach, using information gathered from limited investigations of the amounts of waste being handled in a certain area and extrapolating these results to give a national figure. It will be readily appreciated that the potential for error in the 'output' approach is also considerable.

3.2.3   Regional arisings

Our estimates of current demolition and construction waste arisings are based on information available in each Member State. We have developed regional estimates of arisings on a straightforward population basis. We would point out that this approach will tend to understate arisings in predominantly urban regions and overstate arisings in predominantly rural regions.

3.2.4   Forecasts of future arisings

In developing forecasts of future waste arisings, consideration was given both to the input and output approaches as described above.

The information generally available on the types and ages of structures standing in the Community is scarce. Any attempt at forecasting future levels of construction or demolition activity would be fraught with danger, as during any national economic change, the construction industry is usually that sector which is most affected. We therefore decided that in spite of the lack of adequate data, the input technique would be the most preferable approach to take.

23

It will be seen that we have based forecasts of demolition waste arisings on statistics of cement deliveries and brick production. Brick and concrete constitute well over 90% of the weight of construction materials used in the Community. Our forecasts show the quantities of materials expected to arise from demolition, assuming that structures stand only for a certain length of time. They do not take account of particular national trends, e.g. in Denmark and Italy, where there is very little demolition at the present time due to preferences for rehabilitation. These preferences tend to be temporary, as eventually rehabilitation must give way to demolition for reasons of safety, health or changes in the requirements of buildings (larger rooms, increased surface area, etc.).

Forecast arisings of steel and aluminium from demolition have been obtained in a similar manner to forecasts of brick and concrete arisings.

3.2.5 Appendices

In the following sections which deal with estimates of current arisings we have removed all detailed information to the Appendix in order to make the text more concise. References to tables beginning with the prefix 'A' refer to those tables which appear in the Appendix, thus Table A.1(a) refers to Table (a) in Appendix 1, Table A.2(c) refers to Table (c) in Appendix 2, etc.

3.3 Wastes arising from new construction work

3.3.1 Introduction

Waste materials arising from new construction (mostly earthworks from excavation work) are normally buried on site if the site is large enough to accommodate them prior to paving and landscaping. On smaller sites, in urban areas, this debris is usually taken away for tipping.

It is impossible to accurately quantify the amount of such wastes that require disposal within the Community. Only in Germany, where there is a requirement that all transport of waste materials be monitored (7), is there a reasonable estimate of these materials. In the other Member States, we have had to base our estimates on whatever information is available, and as much of this information is of a subjective, local nature, there is obviously considerable scope for error.

3.3.2 National approaches

In Belgium, Ireland and Italy, we have derived our estimates of waste arisings from new construction work on work carried out on this subject in Europe and elsewhere. One study (6) estimated the quantity of debris requiring removal from the site for different types of buildings. These data are reproduced in Table A.1(a). For each of these countries, information was obtained of the number and type of new buildings constructed, and total waste arisings from new construction were thus estimated.

In France and in the U.K., information was provided by various
local and regional authorities on the wastes disposed of at public
and private tipping sites in their areas.

In the Netherlands, the national statistical office (CBS) has
estimated the quantity of excavation wastes generated, although
it is not known what proportion of this requires disposal at
tipping sites.

We were unable to gain any information on the quantity of construction wastes that are generated in Luxembourg or Denmark.

Table 3.3(a)

EEC SUMMARY TABLE : ESTIMATED QUANTITY OF WASTES GENERATED ANNUALLY BY
NEW CONSTRUCTION WORK

Country	Year of Estimate	Quantity 1000t	Kg per inhabitant per year
Belgium	1976	1158	118
Denmark	–	N/A	N/A
France*	1978	20,000	380
Germany**	1975	36,000	582
Ireland***	1976	350	112
Italy***	1976	2000	36
Luxembourg***	1976	39	15
Netherlands**	1976	3000	218
United Kingdom**	1977	23,000	410
EEC	–	85,547	328

Notes

*   Average figure of estimates given in Appendix A.1.3

**   Basis: Waste arriving at disposal sites

***   From new residential construction only

Detailed information on the technique used in the estimations in each country is given in Appendix 1, and a summary of our estimates is shown in Table 3.3(a).

3.4 Waste arisings from demolition

3.4.1 Basis of estimates

Two basic approaches have been used in the estimations:

i.   Waste materials that are presently disposed of at landfill sites in the Community have been quantified where this information is available.

ii.   Total materials that are generated by demolition activity have been estimated in all other countries.

Estimates of type i. relate to materials tipped at landfill sites, and are applicable to the estimates given for Germany, the Netherlands and the United Kingdom.

Estimates of type ii. relate to materials arisings prior to any recovery action. This basis has been used for all of the other countries. These estimates require to be adjusted to make them net of any recovery action.

3.4.2 Quantity of material originating from demolition

Table 3.4(a)		
ESTIMATED QUANTITY OF DEMOLITION WASTES GENERATED IN THE EEC		
Country	Year of Estimate	Quantity of material generated by demolition (000 tonnes per year)
Belgium	1975	752
Denmark*	1978	108
France	1977	10,400
Germany***	1975	36,000
Ireland**	1976	40
Italy	1977	741
Luxembourg	1975	9
Netherlands***	1976	4,000
United Kingdom***	1978	20,000
EEC		72,050

Notes

*   Excludes industrial demolition

**   Residential demolition only

***   Wastes for disposal

In those Member States in which qualitative information on total demolition waste arisings is not readily available we separated demolition activity into two sectors, <u>residential</u> demolition and <u>non-residential</u> demolition. The principal reasons for taking such an approach in the analysis are:

- to provide estimates for waste arisings from residential demolition, even though data may not be available on which to base estimates of waste arisings from non-residential demolition;

- to provide data on which to base estimates of compositions. The average age of demolition of residential buildings is significantly higher than for non-residential buildings. It thus follows that the proportion of brick and concrete wastes generated by demolition will be different for each sector.

Information on the particular technique used to quantify demolition waste arisings in each country is given in Appendix 2, as are the estimated arisings of this waste. Table 3.4(a) summarises this information.

3.5 <u>Quantity of wastes for disposal</u>

In Belgium, Denmark, France, Ireland, Italy and Luxembourg, the quantity of waste <u>generated</u> by demolition has been calculated. In order to assess the amount of material that requires <u>disposal</u> in these countries, two influences in particular require consideration:

- the quantity of materials <u>recovered</u> in each country must be taken into account;

- the quantity of wastes originating from sources other then demolition or new construction must be included in the estimates.

3.5.1 <u>The amount of materials currently reclaimed</u>

As seen in Section 2.4.1, the most significant materials reclaimed from demolition wastes are ferrous and non-ferrous metals, timber and demolition rubble.

- Reclamation of <u>non-ferrous</u> metals can be considered as approaching 100% in view of their high value.

- For <u>ferrous metals</u>, it is assumed that the only portion that is not recovered is the steel contained in reinforced concrete. It is further assumed that every tonne of reinforced concrete contains 20kg of reinforcing steel*.

---

* Average figure used by demolition contractors in the Federal Republic of Germany.

By analysis of data for those countries in which we have been able to distinguish between reinforced and total concrete arisings (see Appendix 3), we estimate that in all countries other than teh Federal Republic of Germany, arisings of plain concrete in demolition waste are presently about twice as high as those of reinforced concrete. In the Federal Republic of Germany, the large numbers of relatively modern buildings and structures demolished (i.e. post 1930) results in greater arisings of reinforced than plain concrete.

Table 3.5(a) contains our estimates of the quantity of ferrous material contained in reinforced concrete wastes in the EEC.

Table 3.5(a)		
ESTIMATED QUANTITY OF UNRECLAIMED FERROUS MATERIAL ARISING FROM DEMOLITION		
Country	Arisings of reinforced concrete (000 tonnes)	Unreclaimed ferrous material (000 tonnes)
Belgium	92	2
Denmark	N/A	N/A
France	970	20
Federal Republic of Germany	6,300	126
Ireland	2.5	0.05
Italy	45	1
Luxembourg	0.5	0.01
Netherlands	1,050	21
United Kingdom	3,000	60
EEC	11,460	230

In Figure 3.9(b) we have estimated total arisings of ferrous material as approximately 2 million tonnes per annum, and about 1.8 million tonnes are therefore presently reclaimed.

-      For timber, we have assumed that 20% of all timber arising from demolition in the Community is recovered by the demolition contractor for re-sale or re-use within the construction industry. This factor was estimated earlier in Section 2.4.2.

  From the information contained in Appendices 2 and 3, the total quantity of wood wastes requiring disposal in the Community is thus estimated at approximately 1.5 million tonnes each year, and a further 400,000 tonnes per year are reclaimed.

- For <u>demolition rubble</u>, we estimate that approximately 20-25% of total arisings may be used for a specific purpose by the construction industry. This figure is based on our discussions with demolition contractors and transport companies throughout the Community.

3.5.2   <u>Wastes arising from sources other than demolition or new construction</u>

<u>Wastes arising from new civil and hydraulic engineering works</u>

The requirement for disposal of these wastes is not believed to be significant. Although the quantity of material generated can be very considerable, in the majority of cases it is almost wholly re-used on site.

<u>Wastes from repair, rehabilitation and reconstruction</u>

Waste materials generated by repair, maintenance and reconstruction are not normally re-used on site, and are invariably disposed of at landfill sites. Under this heading are included bituminous, asphalt and concrete wastes from road repair and reconstruction, and general demolition rubble from the rehabilitation of housing, or the reconstruction of non-residential buildings. Quantification of such wastes is virtually impossible, as they are dependent upon the <u>type</u> of work, and more importantly the <u>degree</u> of work undertaken. In housing rehabilitation for example, the amount of work can vary from a very small job, such as replacing a door or window frame, to a case in which the whole of the interior of the building is stripped out and re-built.

<u>The significance of wastes arising from repair, maintenance and reconstruction</u>

In order to gain some information on the significance of these wastes in relation to total <u>demolition</u> waste arisings, we estimated the quantity of waste materials <u>likely</u> to be generated by residential rehabilitation and non-residential reconstruction, and related this to the amount of waste materials resulting from demolition for two countries.

In Denmark, national policy favours rehabilitation of housing rather than demolition and new construction. Presently, some 3250 dwellings are rehabilitated each year compared with about 1000 demolitions (8). We assumed that rehabilitation of a typical dwelling unit* would generate ½ tonne of timber, and perhaps a further tonne of hard material (mainly roofing tiles and brickwork). The rehabilitation of housing would thus generate about 5000 tonnes of waste compared with over 55,000 tonnes from demolition.

A similar exercise was undertaken for Belgium, and it was estimated that waste arisings from housing rehabilitation would be

---

*   See Appendix A.2.2 for information on the typical dwelling unit in Denmark.

Table 3.5(b)

ESTIMATES OF DEMOLITION AND CONSTRUCTION WASTES THAT REQUIRE DISPOSAL IN THE EEC EACH YEAR

Country	Construction Waste	Demolition Waste (000 tonnes)			Rehabilitation and Reconstruction Waste (000 tonnes)	Demolition and Reconstruction Waste for Disposal	
		Total Arisings	Materials recovered rubble	timber		Total (000 tonnes)	Per capita kg/inhabitant
Belgium	1,158	750	150	3	75	670	49
Denmark	N/A	108	22	2	11	95	19
France	20,000	10,400	208	83	104	10,200	193
Germany*	36,000	36,000	N/A	N/A	N/A	36,000	582
Ireland	350	40	8	small amount	4	36	12
Italy	2,000	741	150	15	74	650	12
Luxembourg	39	9	2	small amount	1	8	22
Netherlands*	3,000	4,000	N/A	N/A	N/A	4,000	293
United Kingdom*	23,000	20,000	N/A	N/A	N/A	20,000	357
EEC	85,547	72,050	540**	103**	269	71,700	277

*   Based on the quantity of wastes arriving at landfill sites.

**   Excludes material recovered in Germany, Netherlands and the United Kingdom.

approximately 30,000 tonnes per year, compared with between 300,000 and 400,000 tonnes each year from demolition. Some information concerning the numbers of non-residential buildings reconstructed is also available for Belgium and assuming a figure of 10 tonnes of waste generated per building, it was estimated that wastes from this source currently account for approximately 40,000 tonnes per year, compared to about 400,000 tonnes yearly from non-residential demolition.

In those countries in which estimates of demolition waste arisings have been based on the number of demolitions, rather than on the amount of waste material arriving at a landfill site, we have therefore assumed that waste arisings from rehabilitation and reconstruction are 10% of total demolition waste arisings.

3.5.3   The total quantity of construction and demolition waste that requires disposal in the EEC is thus as estimated in Table 3.5 (b).

3.6   The composition of demolition wastes

3.6.1   We have used three main techniques for determining the composition of wastes arising in each country from demolition work:

-         For those countries in which the majority of residential demolition is of a particular type of dwelling, the materials used in construction have been identified and quantified. Estimates of compositions of waste from residential demolition have thus been obtained in Belgium and Luxembourg, Denmark, Ireland and the United Kingdom.

-         The results of national studies have been used where they are available. In the Netherlands for example, the Stichtung Verwijdering Afvalstoffen recently estimated the composition of demolition and construction waste arriving at landfill sites (9), and in the United Kingdom the Building Research Establishment conducted a postal survey of demolition contractors and estimated the quantity and composition of wastes handled (10).

-         Where no other relevant information is available, the results of discussions with demolition contractors and landfill operators in particular areas have been taken as being representative of the composition of national demolition waste arising.

3.6.2   We have not distinguished between the composition of wastes arising from demolition, and wastes arising from repair, rehabilitation or reconstruction. In the previous section it was stated that the latter wastes are impossible to identify because of the wide variations that occur at source, variations that are of both a qualitative and quantitative nature. Although it can be stated that wastes of this type will contain a greater proportion of non-structural materials (namely timber from window-frames, doors and floorboards, sand-lime bricks and plaster board, broken tiles, fittings, etc.) than wastes from demolition, it is not possible to further quantify the arisings of each individual material.

Table 3.6(a)

THE ESTIMATED COMPOSITION OF DEMOLITION WASTES IN THE EEC

Country	Quantity '000 tonnes per year	Composition % by weight			
		masonry	concrete	timber	steel*
Belgium	670	53	43	2	.3
Denmark**	100	92	–	8	N/A
France	10,200	60	30	3	.2
Germany	36,000	64	33	2	.35
Ireland***	40	70	20	2.5	.1
Italy	650	72	15	8	.15
Luxembourg	10	53	43	2	.1
Netherlands	4,000	59	24	6	.5
United Kingdom	20,000	44	52	1	.3
EEC	71,670	57	37	2	.3

*   Calculated from data of Table 3.5(a).

**   Excludes demolition of industrial buildings and structures.

***   From residential demolition only.

We have therefore assumed that waste materials generated by repair, rehabilitation or reconstruction work arise in similar compositions to wastes from demolition.

Details of the techniques used for the determination of the composition of demolition wastes in each country are included in Appendix 3.

Table 3.6(a) summarises the information of Appendix 3, taking into account the quantities of timber and steel reclaimed (see Section 3.5.1).

It can be seen that the proportion of unreclaimed ferrous material in the waste is highest in the Netherlands, Germany, the United Kingdom and Belgium. This reflects the significance of arisings of reinforced concrete wastes in these countries.

<u>Regional estimates of demolition and construction waste arisings</u>

As explained in the introductory paragraphs of this section, we have estimated current regional arisings on a straightforward population distribution. We have, however, made some exceptions to this approach:

-       <u>In Italy</u>, statistics are available whereby regional waste arisings may be calculated in a similar manner to national arisings, and it is therefore not necessary to rely upon a staightforward population distribution for estimating regional arisings. Some interesting observations are apparent from the derived data (see Table A.4(f)).

Firstly, the per capita production of demolition waste is very low compared with most of the other Member States (see Table 3.5(b)). By comparison, demolition activity in Italy is less than 4% of the activity in the United Kingdom, and only about 2% of the activity in Germany. Part of the explanation can be found in the generally low level of activity of the building industry, but it is probable that the national law controlling the demolition of buildings constructed before the Second World War is also a contributing influence.

Secondly, it is shown that demolition waste arisings based on a straightforward population basis are not at all uniform across the country. As mentioned in the introductory paragraphs of this section, it was not expected that this would be the case, but neither did we expect to find variations such as are shown in Table A.4(f) - from 0.4 to 33kg per inhabitant per year.

The situation can probably be explained by the follo-wing. Approximately 75% of all residential buildings and 65% of non-residential buildings were demolished by cause of 'accidental' destruction (fire, industrial contamination, earthquake, etc.) during the years investigated, and the amount of 'planned' demolition was thus negligible (11). And although it is doubtful whether such high proportions of buildings were demo-lished by 'accidental' causes, per capita waste arisings in such a situation would be expected to vary regionally.

-       <u>In Berlin</u>, all waste arisings are carefully monitored, and full quantitative data are available on arisings of demolition waste (12). The composition of demolition wastes is assumed to be similar to that of demolition wastes in the rest of the country. We have therefore sub-tracted the amount of waste known to arise in Berlin from the national figure, and have apportioned other regional arisings on a population basis.

-       <u>In the Netherlands</u>, the results of four quantitative studies of demolition and construction waste are available. Two of these studies monitored waste arisings in the densely populated south western part of the country, whilst the other two measured national arisings. It can be seen from Table A.2(d) that although per capita arisings are higher in the south west than in the country as a whole, a national estimate based on data from the south west would not have been widely dissimilar from the 'true' figure.

- In the United Kingdom we attempted to make allowance for two regions in which demolition activity might be expected to be particularly high.

  In Northern Ireland, terrorist activity in recent years has resulted in unusually large quantities of demolition and construction wastes, and in Scotland, the high proportion of regional aid that has been granted in recent years was also expected to have increased construction and demolition activity. It was in fact shown that residential demolition activity in Northern Ireland and in Scotland was more than twice as great as in England and Wales (see Table A.4(h)(i)).

  The estimated regional distribution of demolition and construction wastes is shown for each country in Appendix 4.

3.8 Confidence limits for estimates of waste arisings

It is difficult to state degrees of confidence for all of the estimates given, as these wastes are very rarely monitored. Only for Germany and in the Netherlands can one state a reasonable degree of confidence, as these figures are the result of one or more national surveys.

In the United Kingdom, our data are in agreement with those suggested during the study by contractors, and with those reported in the literature. In 1976, Nixon (13) estimated a total tonnage of 21-23 million tonnes of demolition waste, of which about 4 million tonnes were generated from residential demolition.

In Belgium, the operators of the major industrial waste tipping sites in the Brussels area suggested that approximately 377,000 tonnes of inert waste were tipped in 1977 (mostly construction and demolition material, but also including household fittings and mixed factory waste). Also in Belgium, a study undertaken in 1974 by the "Conseils Economique de Flandre et de Bruxelles" (14) estimated the per capita arisings of demolition and construction wastes for disposal to be 0.108 tonnes per year, which suggests total arisings of just over one million tonnes. Our estimate of total demolition and construction wastes (1.83 million tonnes in 1975 - Table 3.5(b)) is significantly higher than this figure, although our estimate for waste arisings from the Brussels area (220,600 tonnes - Table A.4(a)) is somewhat less than the estimate for total inert waste given by the tip operators. We therefore judge our estimates for waste arisings in Belgium to be of the correct order.

In France, our estimates of demolition waste arisings are in good agreement with information given in the literature. In 1973, the "Ministère de l'Industrie et de la Récherche" and the "Ministere de la Qualité de la Vie" requested the "Centre Technique du Bois" (CTB) to undertake a study of the quantities of different types of timber wastes. It was found that a total of 500,000 tonnes of timber wastes resulted from demolition work in 1974 (15). This figure is similar to that estimated in Table A.4(c).

In 1976, Primel and Tourenq of the "Laboratoires Central des Ponts et Chaussées" discussed the use of waste materials in road construction (16). They reported that the annual production of demolition waste and of bituminous and concrete wastes was approximately 20 million tonnes/year, although no references were given for this information.

In 1974, an inter-ministerial working group reported that in the Parisian region, about 13 million m^3 (17 million tonnes) of building and construction wastes are deposited each year (17). On a straightforward population basis, this suggests a national figure of about 90 million tonnes annually, which is approximately three times our estimates.

The difference is one of definition; our estimate of total demolition and construction waste (30 million tonnes per year – Table 3.5(b)) is of wastes disposed of to tipping sites, whilst the larger estimate is for total materials handled, most of which are excavation wastes used on site, or used to construct embankments, as surface material, etc.

In the remaining countries we have no other information with which to compare our estimates. However, we believe that those figures given for the other countries may be rather conservative, particularly as we have been unable to assess waste production from civil and hydraulic engineering work in these countries.

Forecasts of future arisings

We have based forecasts of future arisings of demolition wastes on statistics of cement deliveries and brick production in each of the Member States of the Community. Concrete and brick constitute well over 90% of the weight of construction materials used in the Community, and forecast arisings of these materials will therefore be representative of total arisings of demolition rubble.

In addition we have also included forecasts of future arisings of steel and aluminium; steel because of the quantity of reinforcing material that is not reclaimed, and aluminium because of the increased usage of this relatively high value material in new construction.

Demolition rubble

We have classified structures into three basic types and have assumed an average lifetime for each category. These assumptions and categories are given in Table 3.9(a).

Table 3.9(a)		
AVERAGE LIFETIMES OF STRUCTURES		
Category	Sector	Assumed lifetime of structure (years)
Short-life	Industrial	40
Medium-life	Housing, commercial, agricultural	70
Long-life	Schools, hospitals, civil engineering	100

In order to obtain forecasts of waste materials arising from demolition based on an input basis as explained in the introductory paragraphs of this section, we require to know what proportion of total building materials goes into each of these sectors. Information on this does not exist for the Community as a whole. However, statistics are available in France concerning the deliveries of cement to various sectors of the construction industry (18).

We have assumed that:

i.   the proportions for cement deliveries are applicable to total materials deliveries;

ii.   the proportions for deliveries in 1975 are typical for other recent years;

iii.   the proportions for deliveries in France are similar to those in other Community states.

Discussions held with various construction industry organisations and government departments suggest that the figures obtained might be viewed as typical throughout the Community. From these data we have determined the proportionate lifetime of structures in each of the three sectors, i.e.:

        20% of structures have a lifetime of 40 years
        50% of structures have a lifetime of 70 years
        30% of structures have a lifetime of 100 years

In order to estimate arisings of demolition wastes in the future, knowledge of construction materials production dating back over the last 40-100 years is required to take account of the assumed lifetimes of different structures. Unfortunately, however, such data are not available. Cement statistics are available since 1920. Annual production figures for other materials were not generally measured until very much later. Data on deliveries of all of the major building materials is available for the United

Kingdom which indicates that for the year 1948 and 1976, brick and concrete accounted for 96% and 97% of the total weight of materials respectively (19).

Table 3.9(b)

PRODUCTION OF BRICKS AND CONCRETE : EEC - 1920-1972

Year	Bricks[a] million tonnes	Concrete[b] million tonnes	Brick and Concrete million tonnes
1920	55[c]	49.5	104.5
1925	55[c]	103.2	158.2
1930	55[c]	131.7	186.7
1932	55[c]	109.4	164.4
1935	55[c]	156.4	211.4
1938	55[c]	208.9	263.9
1947	55[c]	121.2	176.2
1950	55[c]	213.9	268.9
1955	55	343.1	396.1
1960	58	456.2	514.2
1965	59	638.6	697.6
1970	53	801.2	854.2
1972	55	853.7	908.7

Notes

a   Basic source: Annual Bulletin of Housing and Building Statistics for Europe - 1963, 1969, 1976.

b   Source: World Cement Market in Figures. Assumes 85% of cement is used for concrete manufacture and that $1m^3$ of concrete contains 330kg cement, and weighs 2.4 tonnes.

c   Estimates - see text.

Table 3.9(c)

FORECASTS OF DEMOLITION WASTE ARISINGS IN THE MEMBER STATES OF THE EUROPEAN COMMUNITY

Country	B&L		DK		F		G		IR		I		NL		UK		EEC	
Year	Brick	Con-crete	Brick	Con-crete	Brick	Con-crete	Brick	Con-crete	Brick	Con-crete	Brick	Con-crete	Brick	Con-crete	Brick	Con-crete	Brick	Con-crete
1980	4.3	3.5	1.5	1.0	4.5	10.8	12.7	16.3	.02	0.5	8.9	11.3	4.4	2.3	15.8	9.3	52	55
1985	4.3	3.1	1.5	.9	4.5	9.5	12.7	14.2	.02	0.4	8.9	9.8	4.4	2.0	15.8	8.1	52	48
1990	4.3	4.3	1.5	1.2	4.5	13.4	12.7	20.1	.02	0.6	8.9	13.9	4.4	2.8	15.8	11.5	52	68
1995	4.3	7.7	1.5	2.2	4.5	23.8	12.7	35.8	.02	1.1	8.9	24.8	4.4	5.1	15.8	20.5	52	121
2000	4.3	10.4	1.5	2.9	4.6	31.9	12.9	47.9	.02	1.4	9.1	33.2	4.4	6.8	16.1	27.4	53	162
2005	4.3	13.6	1.5	3.8	4.6	42.0	12.9	63.0	.02	1.9	9.1	43.7	4.4	8.9	16.1	36.0	53	213
2010	4.3	18.0	1.5	5.1	4.5	55.3	12.7	83.2	.02	2.5	8.9	57.6	4.4	11.8	15.8	47.5	52	281
2015	4.3	16.8	1.5	4.7	4.5	51.6	12.7	77.5	.02	2.4	8.9	53.7	4.4	11.0	15.8	44.3	52	262
2020	4.3	19.3	1.5	5.4	4.5	59.5	12.7	89.4	.02	2.7	8.9	61.9	4.4	12.7	15.8	51.0	52	302

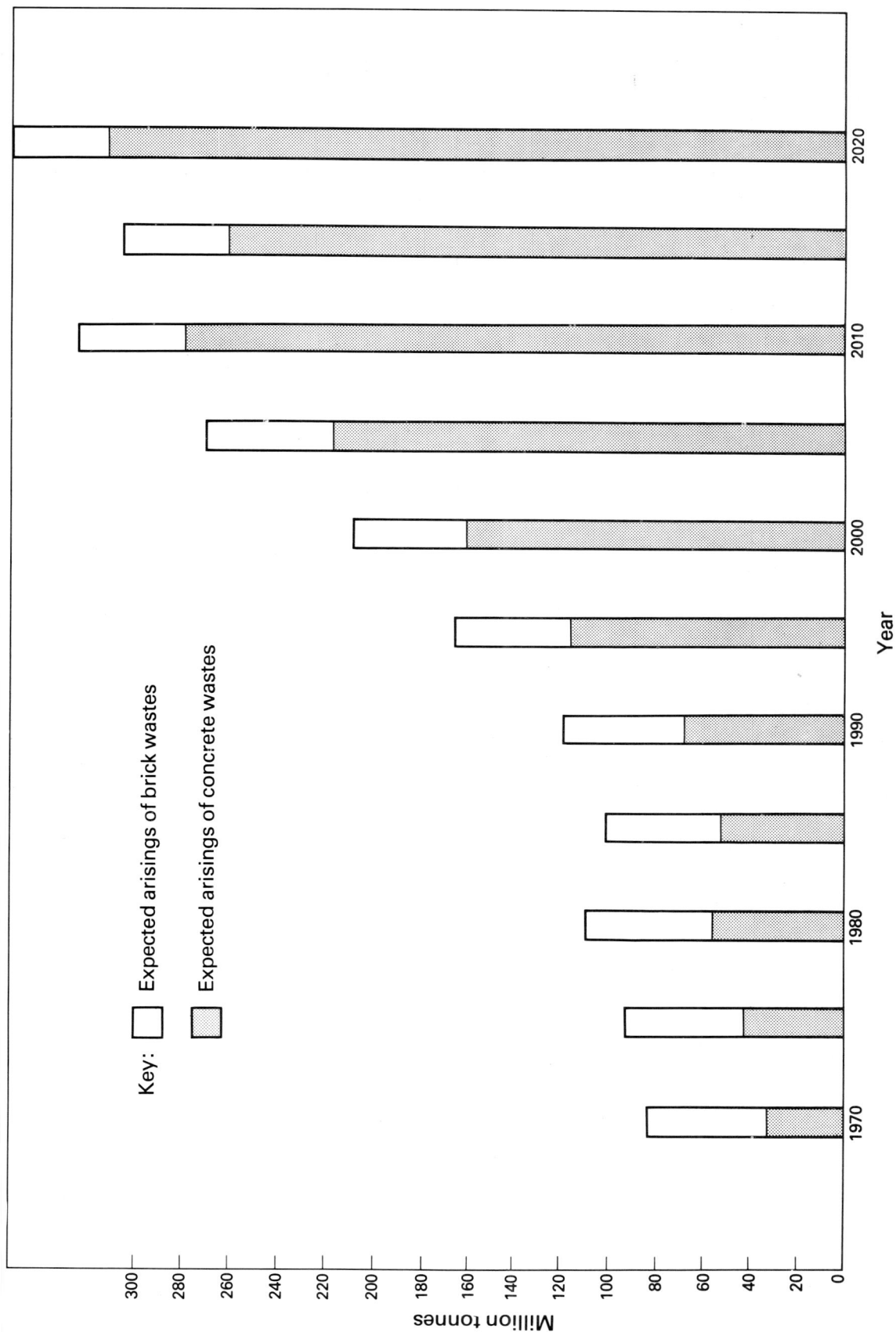

Figure 3.9(a) EXPECTED ARISINGS OF DEMOLITION WASTES IN THE EEC

Key:

☐ Expected arisings of brick wastes

▨ Expected arisings of concrete wastes

We have made similar studies for the other Community Member States, but lack of data, particularly concerning timber and steel used in construction, prevents the degree of accuracy that is obtainable for the U.K. However, the limited information we have suggests that brick and concrete have represented well over 90% by weight of all construction materials, certainly since the early 1950's, in every Member State of the EEC.

Our forecasts of future arisings of wastes from demolition are therefore to be based on these two materials. Data for brick production and deliveries exists in all countries since 1954, and the production of bricks in the Community has remained essentially stable since that date at an annual rate of approximately 55 million tonnes (20).

We were informed by a leading brick manufacturer in the U.K. that pre-war brick production was not significantly different to the early post-war years. We have therefore assumed that brick production in the EEC prior to 1954 was at a similar figure. Based on this assumption, we have compiled information on brick and concrete production in the EEC since 1920 (see Table 3.9(b)).

By apportioning the data given in Table 3.9(b) for the three different categories of structures, it is possible to obtain quantities of brick and concrete wastes that may be expected to arise from demolition. This information is given in Figure 3.9(a) for the EEC as a whole.

Forecasts of future arisings in each of the Member States are made by apportioning total brick and concrete production in the EEC by country. These forecasts are contained in Table 3.9(c).

3.9.2   Steel

As the major fraction of constructional steel is used in industrial structures, we have based our forecasts for future steel arisings on an average lifetime of 40 years as assumed in the previous section.

Data on steel usage in the construction industry are limited. U.K. statistics separate steel used for concrete reinforcement from other steel used in construction, and we have therefore estimated future steel arisings in the EEC from these figures in order to distinguish between easily reclaimable steelwork and steel contained in concrete.

In 1976, the U.K. accounted for 15.8% of total EEC raw steel production (21) and in 1975, the U.K. accounted for 14.9% of the production of steel plate ($\geqslant$ 3mm) in the Community (22). We have assumed that consumption of steel by the construction industry in the U.K. is 15% of that in the EEC.

As the data are not complete for the years 1930-1980 (necessary to forecast arisings between 1970-2020), we assumed various annual growth rates for steel consumption in building and construction. The assumptions are based on the trends shown in the available data, and are as follows:

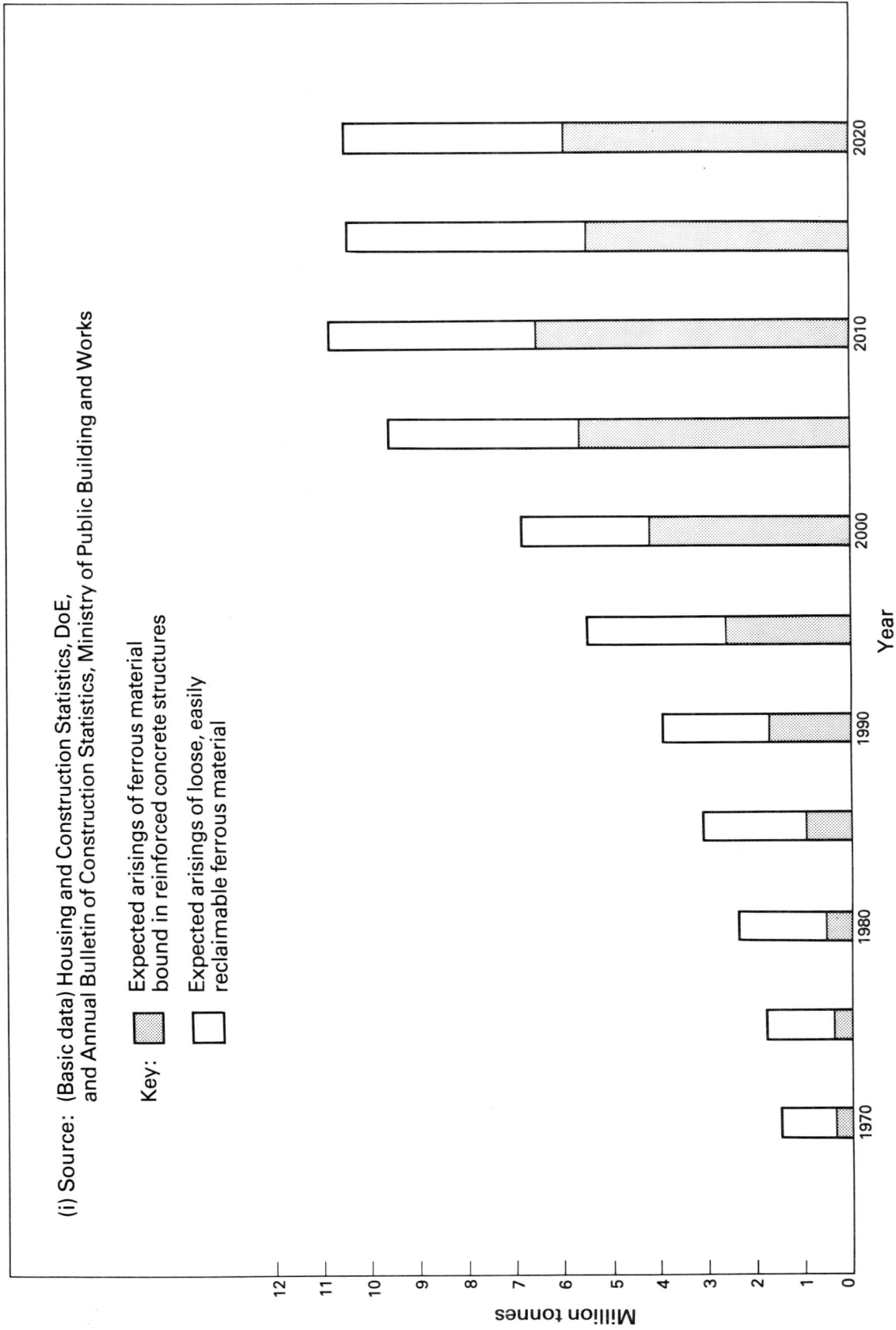

Figure 3.9 (b) EXPECTED ARISINGS OF FERROUS MATERIAL FROM DEMOLITION IN THE EEC (i)

(i) Source: (Basic data) Housing and Construction Statistics, DoE,
and Annual Bulletin of Construction Statistics, Ministry of Public Building and Works

Key:

Expected arisings of ferrous material
bound in reinforced concrete structures

Expected arisings of loose, easily
reclaimable ferrous material

Year

Million tonnes

-       10% growth rate for steel for reinforcing between
        1930 and 1960.

-       7% growth rate for total steel for construction between
        1930 and 1960.

-       0% growth rate for all construction steel between 1976
        and 1980.

Our forecasts of expected steel arisings from demolition are
thus as given in Figure 3.9(b).

3.9.3   Aluminium

Our forecasts for future arisings of aluminium from demolition
are based on an average lifetime of aluminium products used in
buildings and construction of 30 years(23).

Information concerning production of semi-manufactured and foundry
aluminium in the EEC is available since 1946 (24). In order to
forecast aluminium arisings after 2007, we require forecasts of
production between 1978 and 1990. The average annual rate of
growth of production of these materials in the EEC since 1967 has
been 6%, and this figure is used to forecast annual production
figures until 1990.

Data on the end-uses of wrought and cast aluminium in the United
Kingdom are available since 1948 (25, 26).

It is assumed that the proportion of aluminium production used
in the building and construction industry in the U.K. during these
years is representative of aluminium use in this industry in the
whole of the EEC. Based on the above data and assumptions, our
estimates for future arisings of aluminium from demolition are
as given in Figure 3.9(c).

3.9.4   Plastics

Based on sales information supplied by certain national associations representing the plastics and polymer manufacturers, it
would appear that some 1-2 million tonnes/year of plastics are
currently sold to the EEC construction industry. Assuming that
an average historical growth rate for the 1960-80 period for use
of plastics in building was 7% per annum, and for the 1980-90
period the growth will be 3-4% per annum, future annual waste
arisings for plastics in the Member States would be expected to
be of the following order of magnitude:

1990	:	0.3 - 0.6 million tonnes/year
2000	:	1.0 - 2.0 million tonnes/year
2020	:	2.0 - 3.0 million tonnes/year

3.9.5   Glass

No reliable statistics exist for sales of glass to the construction industry.

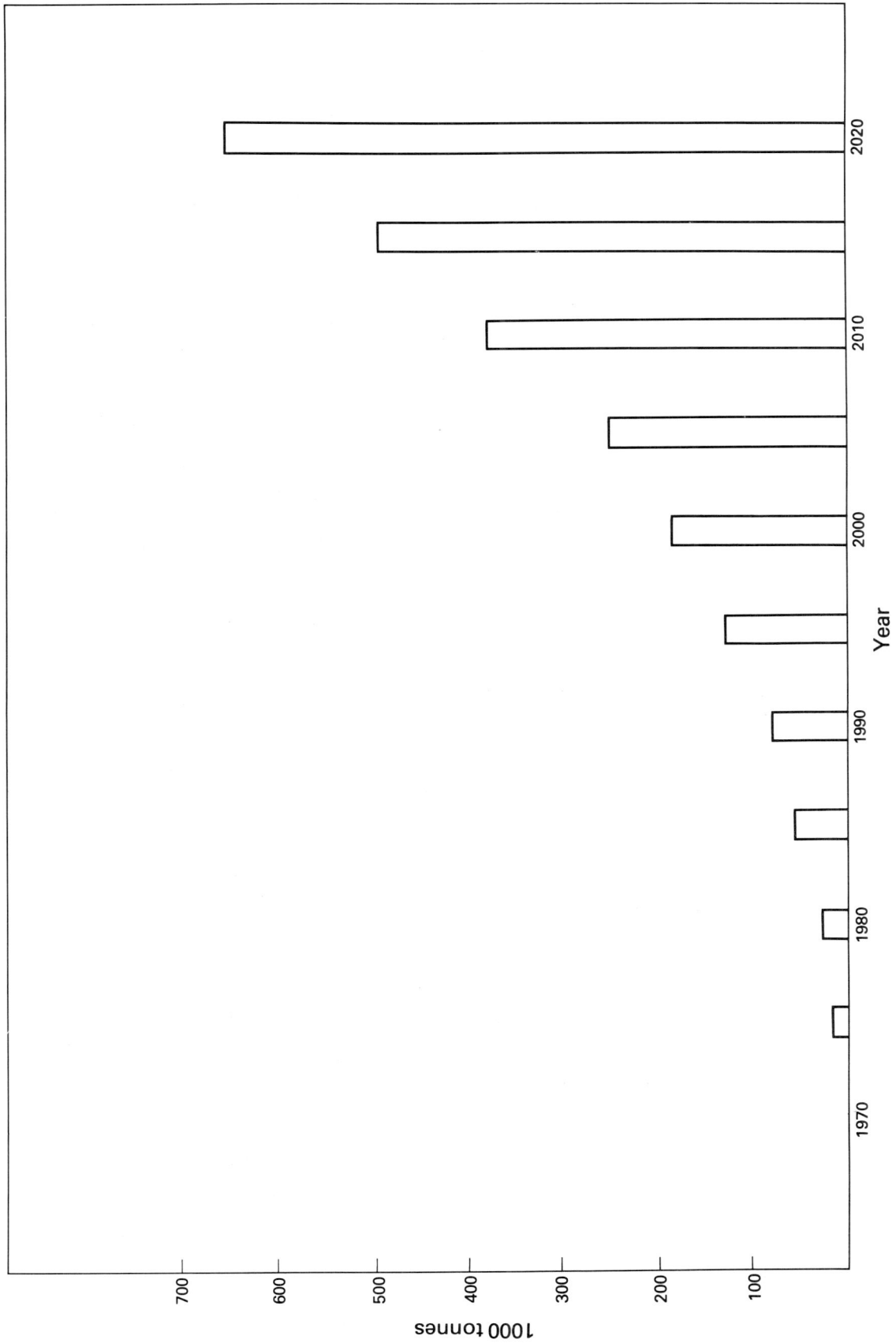

Figure 3.9(c) EXPECTED ARISINGS OF ALUMINIUM FROM DEMOLITION IN THE EEC

4. The economics of handling, recovering and disposing of demolition and construction wastes

4.1 <u>Introduction</u>

4.1.1 <u>Nature and reliability of available data</u>

In Section 4, we examine the costs and (where applicable) benefits of handling and disposing of demolition and construction wastes in various ways. Inevitably, there is considerable difficulty in obtaining reliable, disaggregate data on <u>costs</u> of each stage of processing/handling these wastes. This is an area in which information is generally scarce and where economic data especially are poorly documented and highly variable. Some of the main reasons for this lack of reliable economic information are:

i. many operators do not have a need to develop detailed cost data and, as removing and disposing of the waste will often form only a relatively small part of the value of a demolition/construction contract, 'rule of thumb' approaches to costing this part of the operation are common in the industry;

ii. handling and disposal costs are highly location-specific, such that large variations in costs occur not only between countries in the E.E.C., but also between different localities within a country;

iii. different contractors will have incurred capital costs at different times and under varying financial conditions, and operate under differing circumstances in respect of taxes, labour, regulations, etc. In most cases, it was not possible for us to determine precisely how cost figures quoted were calculated (many being in the nature of rough estimates);

iv. certain activities, for example, separating out valuable and easily accessible materials on-site, applying excavation wastes to the extent feasible for site landscaping or as a fill, are normally carried out as a matter of course, with clear economic advantages to the contractor. Hence, cost data on such activities do not exist as they are not essential for management decision-making by the contractor.

Similar problems are encountered in trying to examine the benefits of recovery from these wastes. From the contractor's point of view, recovering a portion of his waste may confer two kinds of financial benefit, namely:

- possible revenues from the sale of the recovered materials;

- a saving in waste transport and disposal costs.

Alternatively, recovery may be undertaken by an independent processor, in which case part of any realisable benefit to the contractor of a saving in transport and disposal costs may be transferred to the independent processor by means of a payment of a 'drop-charge' by the contractor for being allowed to deliver some or all of his wastes at the processor's plant.

There are considerable difficulties in quantifying costs and financial benefits of waste recovery:

i.   for most materials, there is not a sufficiently regular market to establish firm prices;

ii.   availability of natural aggregate and size of local market will be main determining factors;

iii.   the prices for scrap metals, which can always find an outlet, fluctuate considerably over time and between locations in the EEC;

iv.   transport distances and disposal charges to contractor are highly location specific.

A majority of the cost data was obtained from contractors or local authorities in Member States with a certain amount from published sources. Because of the limited experience of materials recovery from demolition wastes in the EEC, the study also draws on information from the USA. In certain instances, we have built up our own cost estimates on the basis of information supplied and from previous experience gained in the field of waste handling.

It follows that a generalised analysis of the economics of demolition waste handling, disposal and recovery is very difficult. Cost comparisons shown will, therefore, sometimes contain specifically local elements, which will not always be possible to separate. Where general estimates have been derived, they should be seen as approximations.

Costs in this study are expressed in U.S. dollars, converted where necessary from EEC currencies at the exchange rates shown in Table 4.1(a).

Table 4.1(a)		
CURRENCY EXCHANGE RATES USED IN SUBSEQUENT CALCULATIONS		
Country	Currency	Amount of each currency equivalent to one U.S. dollar*
Belgium	Belgian Francs	28.87
Denmark	Kroner	5.06
France	French Francs	4.21
Germany	Deutschmarks	1.83
Ireland	Pounds	0.49
Italy	Lire	831.90
Netherlands	Guilders	1.98
U.K.	Pounds	0.49

* Based on rates prevailing at end-December 1978

4.1.2 Costs and benefits

The costs and benefits associated with demolition wastes can be seen as both direct and indirect.

Direct costs/benefits are those which are tangible and affect the cash flows of demolition waste contractors/processors.

Indirect costs/benefits would not normally enter into the decision making of contractors/processors, but can be seen in the overall social and economic context of the Community.

The main factors are:

i.   the effects on the environment and amenity of transporting and disposing of these wastes;

ii.   conversely, the impact of recovery on environmental pollution and amenity destruction (both from reducing the amount of waste requiring transport and disposal, and reducing the need to extract virgin raw materials);

iii.   the potential value of this material to the Community in terms of savings in imports and intrinsically scarce resources (including energy).

In certain instances, indirect environmental costs have become direct to the extent that controls over noise, air and water pollution, etc., have required expenditure on the part of waste handling and disposal contractors. Often, however, it is not possible to identify values for such environmental costs and benefits, and in any case, depending on the local circumstances they will vary considerably. They are therefore discussed qualitatively in Section 5.5.

4.2   Costs of demolition waste handling and disposal

The handling of demolition and construction wastes typically involves three distinct kinds of activity, namely:

i.   The separation and processing of waste materials and components at the point where these arise (i.e. at the demolition or construction site itself).

ii.   The loading of separated materials and waste into road vehicles and their transport (occasionally via a transfer station) to a storage depot for recovered materials, to a recovered materials dealer/user, or to a disposal site.

iii.   The final disposal of unwanted waste.

A further kind of activity, which is not yet commonly found in the E.E.C., might be the processing and recovery of demolition wastes at a centralised treatment plant. Figure 4.2(a) shows the main possible options for handling demolition and construction wastes, in the form of a flow diagram. A distinction is made between wastes arising from demolition, renovation and construction, and wastes emanating from earthworks and site excavation, in view of their very different composition.

Initial decisions in respect of the handling of the waste belong primarily to the demolition or construction contractor, though, of course, his effective choice may be constrained by conditions laid down in the contract, by conditions attached to the permit to build/demolish, by environmental or safety regulations, etc. However, once the waste leaves the site of origin, the extent to which the demolition/construction contractor is able to control or influence decisions about its subsequent handling varies a great deal, depending upon his own facilities and methods of operation, and local circumstances. A larger contractor, with considerable resources and equipment at his disposal, may operate a transport fleet and be in a position to service his own waste transport needs. He may even, in certain instances, be operating his own landfill site in the vicinity of a major conurbation and will therefore be able to dispose of the waste himself. At the other extreme, a small contractor often will not operate vehicles for removing the waste and will sub-contract for its removal and disposal. Responsibility for the waste may then pass to the sub-contractor, although legislation in some member countries means that the originator of the waste remains responsible for ensuring that the waste is transported and disposed of in a proper manner, even though this is carried out by another party.

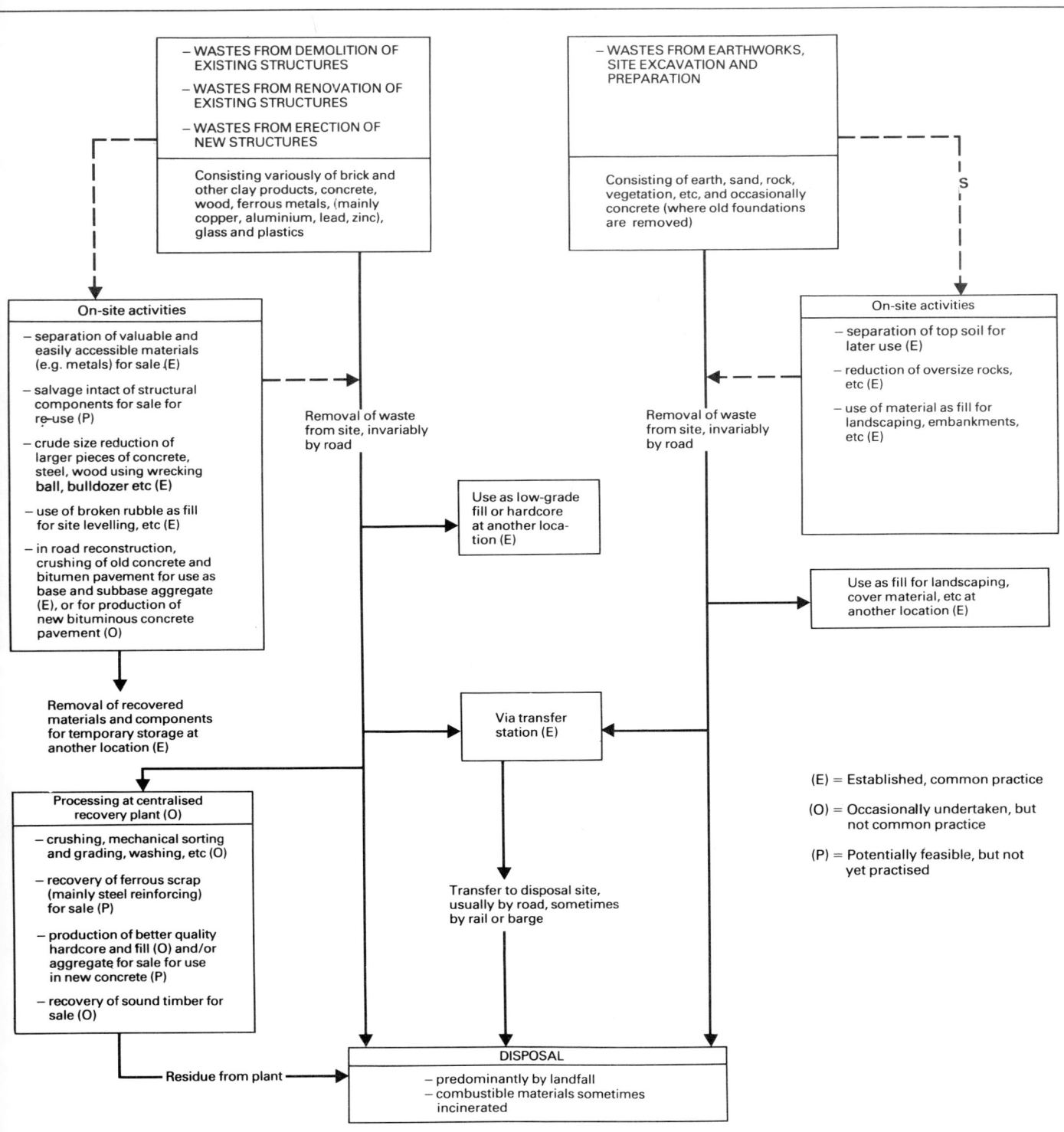

Figure 4.2(a)   SIMPLIFIED FLOW DIAGRAM TO SHOW THE MAIN, POSSIBLE OPTIONS FOR HANDLING DEMOLITION AND CONSTRUCTION WASTES

In considering the economics of waste handling, it is therefore important to realise that decisions affecting handling are rarely totally under the control of the demolition/construction contractor and that several separate organisations are often involved at different stages.

4.2.1   Materials separation

The extent of materials separation and their associated costs will depend on the values of materials, upon their degree of contamination, the type of structure and other operating conditions, such as the time-penalty clauses in demolition contracts. None of the contractors interviewed could provide cost information relating to this activity, and decisions on recovery are based on management judgement and consideration of these factors.

As will be discussed in Section 4.3, most uncontaminated ferrous and non-ferrous metals are recovered. Little or no steel is currently recovered from reinforced concrete as contractors are of the opinion that no satisfactory low cost method exists for separating the materials on site. Also, there are no mechanised methods for recovering materials such as roofing tiles, bricks, stone blocks and timber, whose separation is strongly dependent on the local market.

4.2.2   Size reduction of materials

The costs of size reduction of materials are again very dependent upon the type of material, structural circumstances, the degree of size reduction, the equipment used and site conditions, and contractors were unable to provide quantitative information. An independent German source estimated that finer crushing of concrete could cost around DM25 (US$13) / tonne (27).

4.2.3   On-site materials re-use

Re-use of materials on site, although adding initially to the demolition contractor's costs, offers considerable overall savings through reducing the volume of material to be removed from site. Salvaging of intact steel components and recycling of old bituminous concrete pavement in the new pavement provides the most accessible on-site re-use opportunities. The OECD have reported (4) that recycling of old bituminous pavement can yield cost savings of up to 23% in road construction projects, though our investigations revealed that this activity is much more prevalent in the United States than within the EEC.

4.2.4   Transport of demolition wastes

Wastes from demolition and construction are invariably transported from their site of origin by road. The types of vehicle used may range from the smaller, 2-axle tipping truck or skip-carrier to the much larger articulated, bulk haul truck. The design payload of trucks used for this purpose can vary from a few tonnes up to around 24 tonnes. The effective maximum payload is determined by regulations in each country with respect to vehicle weights, but we are aware that loading in excess of permitted vehicle weights is not uncommon.

50

The costs of operating a vehicle are made up of standing costs (wages, licences, rent and rates, insurance, interest on capital employed) and running costs (fuel, oil, maintenance, depreciation). In addition, there are overhead costs not directly connected with the operation of a particular vehicle (administration, telephone, etc.) and, in the case of a private concern, the operator's profit margin. The way in which these costs are reflected in the cost of transporting a tonne of waste from site of origin to a disposal site or processing plant is a function of:

i. vehicle operating rate;

ii. the nature (particularly density) of the material transported;

iii. the time required for the round trip (including loading and unloading time), which is in turn largely determined by the distance involved and the average speed achievable over the trip.

The rate at which a vehicle is operated depends on several factors: besides the demand for the vehicle's services, factors such as union rules, time for routine servicing and major repairs, regulations governing times when certain vehicles may operate, etc., all impose limitations on the rate at which vehicles may be operated. For the types of vehicle concerned here, normal operating rates could vary over a range of 1,500 - 2,100 hours per year and a typical average might be 1,800 hours per year.

The density of the material carried can be important in determining whether the maximum payload of the vehicle can be achieved. Densities of building and construction wastes vary considerably, but typical densities are:

Unbroken concrete masses (plain and reinforced) - c.2.4 t/m^3

Unbroken brickwork masses - c.1.3 t/m^3

Broken concrete/broken brickwork - c.1.3 t/m^3

Excavation waste/fine rubble - c.1.6 t/m^3

Mixed rubble - c.1.2 t/m^3

Wood (unbroken) - c.0.4 t/m^3

Normally, with most of these materials, there is no problem in reaching the maximum payload of the vehicle within the volume available; in fact, often the maximum payload is reached with a good deal of space to spare (hence the temptation to exceed permitted payloads). However, unbroken debris, despite the higher density of the large masses of material, involves a good deal of voidage when loaded in a vehicle, such that operating payloads for unbroken debris are often significantly lower than the maximum allowed. This demonstrates one of the main reasons why size reduction of materials can yield significant overall savings to the contractor.

From our discussions with contractors, it seems that wastes are rarely transported more than about 60 kms. from site of origin, and within 25 kms. would be typical for much of the waste transported in the Community. Average speeds for trips are strongly influenced by the type of roads on route and traffic congestion. Much demolition and construction waste arises in built-up areas and is transported to sites on the edges of or beyond built-up areas. Over short distances, therefore, there is usually little opportunity for increasing average vehicle speeds much above a certain level but over longer distances improvements in average speeds may be feasible, especially if a motorway or dual carriageway forms part of the journey.

While the factors discussed above are the principal determinants of the cost of transporting wastes by road, other factors may influence the amount a contractor actually has to pay to remove his waste. These include:

- whether the contractor operates his own vehicles, or has to sub-contract;

- the size and duration of a sub-contract;

- the opportunities available for obtaining a return load;

- the effects of any existing tariff regulations (e.g. the Tarif fur den Guternahverkehr mit Kraftfahrzeugen in Germany), etc.

In Appendix 5, we have listed some of the cost figures for transporting demolition wastes by road quoted to us by different demolition and building contractors. It may be seen that the range of transport costs quoted is very large, varying from $0.08-0.39 per tonne per kilometre. Some of the variation in quoted costs will stem from differences in vehicle operating costs (wages, taxes, fuel, etc.) between member countries, but most of the variation is undoubtedly accounted for by the different assumptions underlying the figures and the widely differing operating circumstances (typical loads, distances to tip, etc.) experienced by contractors.

As a check on these costs, and in order to provide some additional insight into demolition waste transport costs, we have calculated typical operating costs for two different sizes of vehicles (8 tonnes and 20 tonnes), and examined how demolition waste transport costs vary according to journey times, distances and the nature of the material transported. The basis and calculation of these costs are shown in Appendix 6.

In Table 4.2(a) we have used the data from Appendix 6 to show for each size of vehicle, the estimated cost for the Netherlands of transporting demolition waste in relation to average vehicle speed and distance to tip. It is estimated that the likely variation in costs throughout other Member States is +10%/-15%. It will be seen from Table 4.2(a) that the range of costs calculated on per tonne/kilometre (one way) basis is similar to that quoted to ERL by contractors.

The trend in transport costs is represented graphically in Figure 4.2(b) and indicates the impact of vehicle size and distance on costs. It will be noted that the smaller vehicle will only have a cost advantage over the 20 tonne truck when a full payload cannot be achieved for the larger vehicle. Also, the rise in costs with distance will normally be less marked than that shown in Figure 4.2(b), as average speeds in the 5-10km range are likely to be considerably less than those in 10-60km range. The dotted lines show, in practice, how transport costs might rise in the 10-40km range.

Table 4.2 (a)				
COST OF TRANSPORTING WASTE IN RELATION TO SIZE OF TRUCK, AVERAGE VEHICLE SPEED, AND DISTANCE FROM SITE OF ORIGIN TO TIP - NETHERLANDS, 1978				
Average speed of vehicle km/hr	Distance to tip km	Cost of Transport in: (i) (ii)		
		8-tonne truck	20-tonne truck	
		$/tonne	$/tonne/ km(one-way)	$/tonne	$/tonne/ km(one-way)
15	5	1.71	0.35	1.00	0.20
	10	2.94	0.29	1.69	0.16
	20	5.37	0.27	3.08	0.16
	30	7.82	0.27	4.47	0.14
	40	10.27	0.27	5.86	0.14
	50	12.71	0.24	7.27	0.14
	60	15.16	0.24	8.65	0.14
30	5	1.39	0.29	0.80	0.16
	10	2.29	0.22	1.29	0.12
	20	4.08	0.20	2.29	0.12
	30	5.90	0.20	3.29	0.10
	40	7.69	0.18	4.27	0.10
	50	9.49	0.18	5.27	0.10
	60	11.29	0.18	6.24	0.10
45	5	1.29	0.27	0.73	0.14
	10	2.06	0.20	1.16	0.12
	20	3.65	0.18	2.02	0.10
	30	5.24	0.18	2.88	0.10
	40	6.84	0.16	3.73	0.10
	50	8.41	0.16	4.59	0.08
	60	10.00	0.16	5.45	0.08

Notes (i)   Assuming truck carries its maximum design payload.
      (ii)   Includes an allowance of 30 minutes on the round-trip time for loading and unloading.

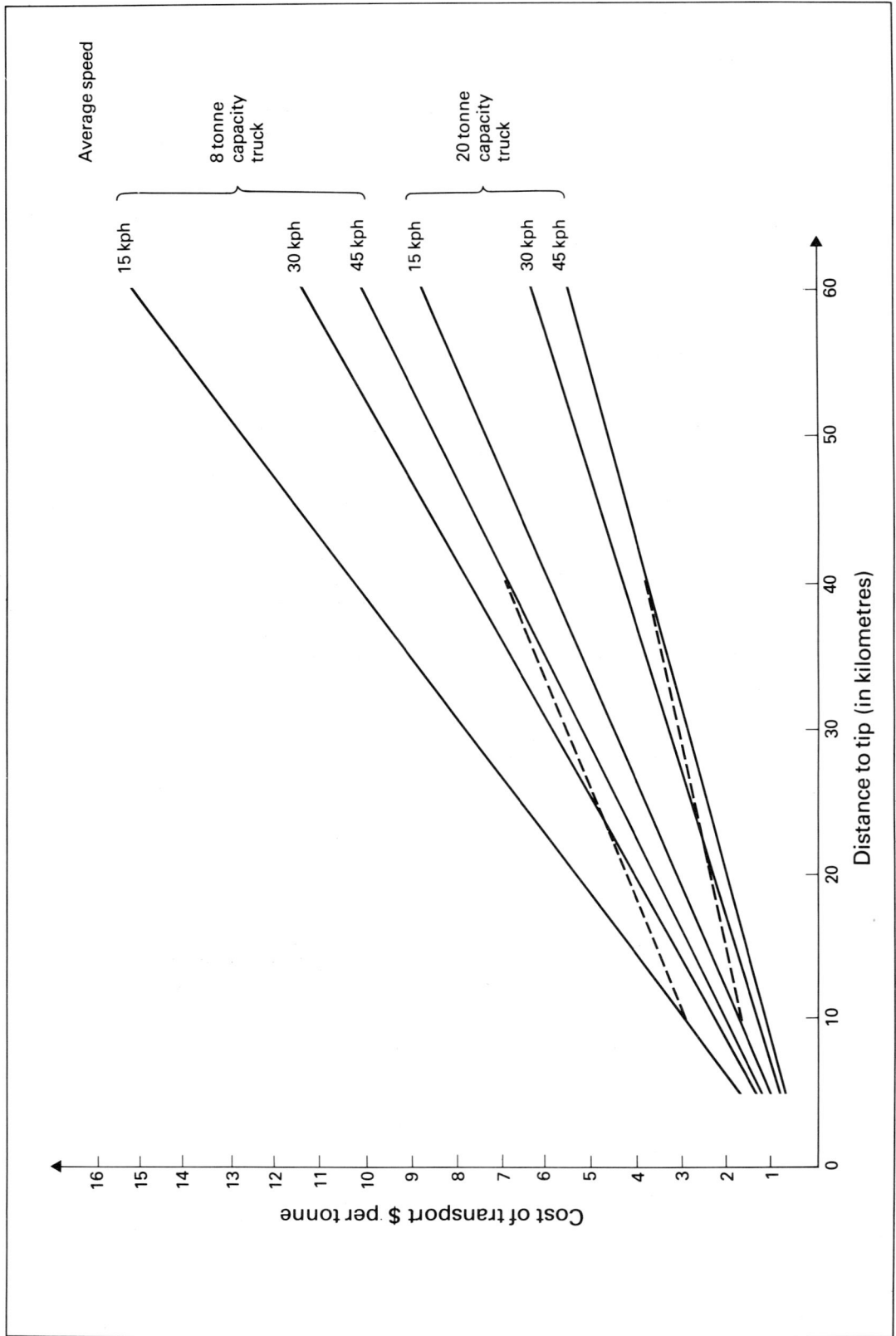

Figure 4.2(b) COST OF TRANSPORTING DEMOLITION WASTE IN THE NETHERLANDS – 1978 (FROM TABLE 4.2(a) AND CONVERTED TO US DOLLARS AT $1 = £ 1.1.98)

The costs shown in Table 4.2(a) and Figure 4.2(b) are based on mixed demolition construction wastes with little inherent voidage. Naturally, where unbroken debris or lower density timber waste is transported, costs per tonne of waste can rise significantly.

Occasionally, demolition wastes are transported via a transfer station, where the material is handled, stored and transported to final disposal using an alternative means of bulk transport, such as barge or train. This is only likely to be economically justified where there are no available disposal tips within 50-60km of the disposal site, where the unit transport cost savings afforded by train, barge, etc., are such as to justify the extra handling stage. For example, in Berlin, large quantities of demolition wastes are transferred to barges for transport to the German Democratic Republic.

4.2.5 Final disposal

Virtually all the demolition and construction waste remaining after any recovery has taken place, is disposed of on land.

The costs of operating landfill sites are highly specific to the site in question and, as such, vary widely throughout the EEC. Very few demolition or construction contractors appear to own or operate their own sites and, consequently, most contractors are more concerned with what they will be charged to tip rather than in what a site actually costs to operate. There are a number of possible reasons why charges for disposing of these wastes may differ radically from the average cost per tonne tipped of operating a site. Some common reasons are:

- mixed and broken building rubble can make a reasonably good cover material for over-laying other tipped wastes and ,where cover material is not readily availabe at the site, the operator may wish to encourage contractors to use his site by charging at a level significantly lower than unit operating costs;

- there may be a local shortage of suitable landfill capacity such that a site commands a premium, and allows the operator to charge at a level significantly above unit operating costs;

- where an operator might be willing to accept waste containing large masses or a high proportion of timber, the problems of handling such waste on a landfill site may mean that charges are set at an appropriately high level.

Hence, aside from variations in costs of a nature related to site development and operation, there are other reasons why charges for tipping waste differ so markedly.

In Table 4.2(b), we have set out some examples of charges for tipping these wastes quoted to us by contractors in different EEC countries. This table shows that charges may range from zero to around $22 per tonne of waste tipped. Charges for delivery to transfer stations are usually much higher, but these naturally reflect a substantial element for transporting the waste to tip, as well as the tipping charge.

55

Table 4.2(b)

EXAMPLES OF TIPPING CHARGES FOR DEMOLITION AND CONSTRUCTION WASTES IN THE EEC (1978)

Country	Locality	Tipping charge quoted $ per tonne	Comment
Belgium	-	1.2	
Denmark	-	0.2-0.4	At land reclamation sites.
Denmark	-	0.4-0.8	At inland tips.
Denmark	-	0.8-1.2	Heavily mixed with timber.
France	Nice	0.1-0.2	
France	Lyon	0.2-0.4	
France	Le Havre	1.4	Concrete, timber, etc.
France	Paris	1.0	Mixed waste.
France	Paris	0.2-0.4	Hardcore, earth.
Italy	-	0.1	
Germany	Vicinity Hamburg	1.6-2.7	
Germany	Ruhr-Emscher	2.9	Local scarcity of land-fill capacity.
Germany	Düsseldorf	2.2-3.3	
Germany	Essen	4.4-5.5	Public site.
Germany	Gelsenkirchen	1.1	Broken material.
Germany	Gelsenkirchen	4.4	Waste with large masses.
Netherlands	-	0.8	
Netherlands	-	0.9-4.0	Unbroken concrete.
U.K.	Berkshire	14.9	Public site.
U.K.	Stafford	0-4.0	
U.K.	Scotland	0-1.0	
U.K.	West Sussex	8.2	

In the two countries where combustible wastes are incinerated (mainly Germany, occasionally in the Netherlands), charges for incineration are understandably much higher than for tipping on land. In the Netherlands, charges range from $20-28 per tonne, while in Germany charges of $22 per tonne and upwards were indicated to us.

4.3   Value of recovered materials

As indicated in Section 2, existing products/materials that may be recovered from demolition/construction wastes are:

-        materials for recycling (applies essentially to metals);

-    items for re-use (structural steel components, bricks, stone blocks, roofing, timber, fittings, etc.);

-    materials for use in lower grade applications.

4.3.1   Materials for recycling

In the case of metals for recycling, scrap metal values broadly reflect the cost of extracting the primary metal from virgin ores. However, the prices of scrap metals are significantly influenced by market considerations, in particular:

-    the demand for finished metals, which in turn is closely related to economic climate;

-    technical processing factors (e.g. electric arc steel making can operate with up to 100% scrap feedstock, whereas oxygen conversion processes are limited to about a 30% scrap feedstock);

-    the amounts and qualities of scrap (including imported scrap) being made available;

-    transport cost considerations.

Table 4.3.(a)		
CURRENT VALUES OF FERROUS SCRAP IN SELECTED E.E.C. COUNTRIES (LATE 1978)		
Country	Type of Scrap	Price quoted in $ per tonne (delivered)
Denmark	"Ferrous scrap"	20 - 30
Germany	"Steel scrap"	50 - 60
Netherlands	"Ferrous scrap"	60 - 70
Netherlands	"Ferrous scrap"	55
Netherlands	"Scrap, depending on quality"	50 - 70
U.K.	"High quality, constructional"	75 - 80
U.K.	"Heavy cast iron"	65 - 70
U.K.	"Mixed ferrous"	40 - 55

In quantitative terms, easily the most important metal recovered from demolition activity is high quality steel scrap for which there is always a demand. The same may be said for scrap non-ferrous metals (copper, lead, zinc, aluminium, and certain alloys), though the amounts available for recovery are very much smaller. Nevertheless, prices of scrap metals do fluctuate significantly, particularly prices of ferrous scrap, the reasons for which are well documented elsewhere (28). As an indication of the current values of ferrous scrap in the EEC, we list some of the prices quoted to us by contractors as being readily obtainable, in Table 4.3(a).

Prices for ferrous scrap delivered to buyers'works in the E.E.C. currently lie in a range of $20-80 per tonne. Most of the ferrous scrap arising from demolition would command prices towards the upper end of this range, in view of its high quality. Contractors were not generally able to give examples of prices for non-ferrous metals, but our inquiries through other sources indicated the following typical values in the E.E.C.:

Copper	–	$900 – 1,300 per tonne (delivered)
Lead	–	$500 – 670 per tonne (delivered)
Zinc	–	$200 – 275 per tonne (delivered)
Brass	–	$700 – 770 per tonne (delivered)
Aluminium	–	$600 – 780 per tonne (delivered)

4.3.2 Items for re-use

The values of re-usable items presently recovered from demolished structures are much more difficult to quantify, as so much can depend on local factors. Any re-usable steel items are readily saleable and will usually fetch a much higher price than if they were sold as scrap. Second-hand bricks, stone blocks, roofing slates and good-condition timber, wherever a local demand exists, can fetch prices of one-third to two-thirds the price of the new items. Some types of fittings can fetch very high prices, because of their rarity or aesthetic value. Table 4.3(b) contains examples of values quoted to us for certain re-usable items.

4.3.3 Materials for low grade applications

The demand for and values of recovered materials for use in lower-grade applications such as hardcore or for fill/cover material are almost exclusively determined by local factors. In these uses, the recovered material (mainly brick and concrete in varying proportions from demolition, or earth and rock from excavation) is substituting for natural aggregates such as gravel, sand and stone. Sometimes where a material of very low quality is required, nearby demolition or excavation contractors are able to supply suitable material which has had little or no processing. Whether or not the contractor is able to charge for, has to give away, or has to pay something for the acceptance of his material, is determined both by what the user would have to pay to obtain natural aggregate and by the amount the contractor would have to pay to dispose of his waste otherwise. Each respectively will usually be broadly aware of the other party's circumstances.

Table 4.3(b)

EXAMPLES OF PRICES OBTAINED FOR RE-USABLE ITEMS RECOVERED FROM DEMOLISHED STRUCTURES (LATE 1978) (i)

Country	Item	Value in $
Belgium	Good condition timber	½-¾ price of new timber.
France	Good condition timber	ca.½ price of new timber.
Germany	Timber joists of max. size 300 x 100 mm	75 per m^3
Germany	Steel joists over 180 mm	150 per tonne (delivered)
Germany	Re-usable electric motors	225 per tonne (delivered)
Germany	Re-usable tubes	90 per tonne (delivered)
Netherlands	Steel beams - re-usable	150-200 per tonne (delivered)
Netherlands	Good condition timber	ca.$\frac{2}{3}$ price of new timber.
Netherlands	Timber joists of max. size 300 x 100 mm	125 per m^3 (average)
Netherlands	Steel joists over 180 mm	250 per tonne average (delivered)
U.K.	Secondhand bricks (hard)	Up to 120 per 1000 bricks
U.K.	Steel beams - re-usable	180 per tonne (delivered)
U.K.	Good condition timber	120 per m^3 average

(i) Obtained from individual contractors and the European Demolition Association.

More critical applications of demolition debris, e.g. as road base or sub-base, normally require sorting, crushing, and grading to varying degrees. The few permanent facilities carrying this out in the EEC are not operated by demolition contractors but by independent companies. Even so, the demand for the processed products of the plants and the prices they command are also closely dependent upon the availability and delivered cost of natural aggregates in the vicinity of the plants.

F.O.B. prices for natural aggregates differ according to country, source and type; our inquiries suggest an EEC range of $2-8 per tonne of aggregate ex-works, with $4-5 per tonne being typical. Transport costs then need to be added to give the delivered price, and some indication of these can be gained from Table 4.2(a) (which dealt with costs of transporting waste), as natural aggregates are at least as dense as most demolition/building wastes and, in most cases, denser. For example, delivery by 20-tonne truck over a distance of 10km with an average speed of 15kph would add around $2 per tonne for transport, while over a distance of 60km with an average speed of 30kph would add around $6 per tonne.

As sources of aggregates adjacent to urban conurbations become increasingly scarce, increasing bulk haul of aggregates by rail is taking place. For example, in 1977 some 7.5 million tonnes of aggregates were transported by rail in the U.K. alone, distances averaging over 150km (29). Clearly transport considerations are a key element in the delivered price of natural aggregates and hence play a key role in determining the price that may be obtained for aggregates recovered from waste. Having made this point, it then becomes extremely difficult to generalise about the values of recovered aggregates. Some broad idea may be obtained from the prices currently charged by operators of the three processing plants visited during the study:

	Price per tonne, ex-works, including Value Added Tax
U.K. plants (Scratchwood and West Drayton):	
- Coarse aggregate	$1.90
- Fine aggregate	$2.20
German plant (Hamburg):	
- Washed rubbed sand (U3)	$3.00
- Fine, crushed brick (<10mm)	$6.90
- Brick grit (3/15mm & 15/30mm)	$15.00
- Coarse brick ballast (60/200mm)	$12.00
- Wall rubble for construction of roads	$4.30

All of the plants, particularly the Hamburg plant, take advantage of the lack of local sites producing natural aggregates.

It appears that recovered aggregates from demolition wastes can compete with natural aggregates in certain circumstances. However, two important factors concerning the demand for recovered aggregates need to be borne in mind:

60

i.   In low-grade applications, material recovered from
        demolition waste is also sometimes competing with other
        waste materials such as pulverised fuel ash, steel
        slags, colliery spoil, etc., which for some uses have
        preferable qualities;

ii.   the demand for aggregates in many localities for such
        applications as base material in road-making, as fill
        or cover material, etc., while significant, is certainly
        not great enough to absorb all the recovered material
        which might be made available from demolition, construc-
        tion or other types of mineral wastes.

This implies that new ways of using such recovered materials
need to be developed, if further recovery from demolition wastes
is not to be constrained by lack of demand. This will be discussed in Section 5.3.

4.3.4   Future trends

1.   Metals

For non-ferrous metals, such as zinc and lead, it is expected that
the future world supply/market balance is likely to lead to increasing real prices for these materials and so will continue to
support their on-site recovery.

Aluminium and ferrous metals, though plentiful in terms of future
supply, are both highly energy intensive in their manufacture.
This will tend to result in a long term rise in the real prices
of these metals, and will also favour the less energy intensive
recycling source for these metals. The economics of recovering
reinforcing steel from concrete should therefore improve.

2.   Re-usable items

Generally, it is to be expected that the financial incentive to
recover these items from demolition waste will be at least as good
in the future as is the current situation.

3.   Low-grade applications

Natural aggregates, generally speaking, are in relatively abundant
supply in the EEC. However, in many areas the sources of supply
adjacent to urban conurbations are becoming increasingly scarce,
so that the transport element in the delivered cost of aggregates
for these areas can be expected to rise in the future as sources
further away are exploited. As the real price of oil is also
expected to rise in the long term, this also is likely to contribute
to increases in the cost of delivered aggregates. Conversely, it
must be recognised that the cost of operating crushing and
mechanical sorting equipment will also be affected by increased
energy costs.

Another factor favouring recovery and processing of rubble to
produce low-grade aggregates is the fact that in some areas of
the EEC, local land-fill sites used for the disposal of solid
waste are becoming less available, partly through public opposition

to the development of such sites. Greater environmental controls over land-fill sites are also increasing the cost of developing and operating such sites, and so will result in increased tipping charges.

4.4 The economics of centralised processing of demolition wastes

4.4.1 Introduction

One conclusion to have come out of the investigations undertaken during this study is that, in future, any significant expansion in the amount of demolition material recovered in the EEC, will need to rely very much more on centralised processing in plants of the type reviewed earlier. This is not to say that processing on-site with mobile equipment would not have an important role. However, in our view, there are several serious obstacles to overcome with on-site processing and recovery on an expanded scale:

-    the processes involved inevitably generate noise, vibration and dust at levels which would be unacceptable in many site locations in urban areas;

-    in many cases, demolition contractors are working to stringent time constraints, such that they have little option but to demolish the structure and clear the site as rapidly as possible;

-    the space required for processing is quite large, and this may not be available at many sites;

-    demolition of small structures may not produce enough material to justify bringing in mobile equipment to process on-site;

-    the equipment needed is quite expensive to buy and, given that many demolition contractors are very small concerns, many could not afford the investment required and may not be able to use the full capacity of the equipment (hiring plant might solve this problem to some extent, but unit processing costs may be further increased).

4.4.2 Existing central processing plants

The number of centralised demolition waste processing plants currently in operation is small. In the EEC, we are aware of several operating in the U.K. and one in Germany. Outside of the EEC, one plant is operating in Switzerland, but the most activity seems to have occurred in the U.S.A. We have inspected, and interviewed the operators of three plants in the EEC, one in Germany and two in the U.K.

Most plant operators are selective about the types of waste they will accept for processing. Many will not accept reinforced concrete, or rubble containing excessive amounts of timber or other non-mineral wastes such as plastics. Some will not accept

waste made up predominantly of concrete (plain). The products
of existing plants may consist of one or more of the following:

- hardcore, for use mainly in road construction;

- aggregate for use as a fill;

- ferrous scrap (mainly from steel reinforcing);

- bricks and stone blocks (for re-use);

- timber.

The last three products are not often recovered. No existing
plant that we are aware of processes all concrete into an
aggregate for use in new concrete. Similarly, the very small
quantities of non-ferrous metals and plastics occurring in waste
by the time it reaches the plant, would make separation and recovery
very costly, and there are real technical problems in sorting these
materials mechanically (see Section 5).

Table 4.4(a)

ESTIMATED 1978 PRODUCTION COSTS OF THREE EEC DEMOLITION WASTE RECOVERY PLANTS

Type of Cost	Hamburg, Rothensburgort, FRG	West Drayton, UK	Scratchwood, UK
	DM	£	£
Capital cost of Plant (installed)	2.5 million	400,000	250,000
Running costs (wages, power, maintenance, etc) per annum	400,000	75,000	50,000
Overhead costs (rent, telephone, administration, etc.) per annum	200,000	20,000	12,000
Average production cost per tonne of aggregate (i)	6.75(ii)	0.90	1.02

Notes: (i) Assumes close to 100% of waste input goes into final products.
Capital costs have been amortised over 15 years at 25% (allows
for debt charges, profit margin and an element for tax).

(ii) The operator of this plant has to pay between DM2-4 per tonne
in order to obtain sufficient of the right types of waste.
This cost needs to be added to the production cost shown.

Appendix 7 lists some existing demolition waste processing plants and shows their main operating characteristics. All of these plants are primarily involved in processing selected types of demolition waste to produce aggregates of various kinds. Only the U.K. plants are willing to handle reinforced concrete, and then only in limited quantities. All the EEC plants are situated on open sites located well away from residential areas, and all rely to different degrees on a local scarcity of natural aggregates to stimulate a demand for their products.

As might be expected, available data on the operating costs of processing plants are limited and often subject to local considerations. In the U.S.A., Stamatia Frondistou-Yannas and Taichi Hoh (both of the Massachussetts Institute of Technology) (30) compared calculated and actual production costs for aggregate at four processing projects. Their data are also presented in Appendix 7, which indicate 1976 costs of producing aggregate from concrete waste of $1.30-1.64/tonne.

The operators of the three EEC plants visited were not willing to reveal details about their operating costs, but we have estimated these from the limited data given to us on equipment costs, manning levels, etc., and from what was seen during visits. Our estimates are presented in Table 4.4(a) and these should be regarded only as very approximate indications of the actual costs for each plant. None of the plants have much in the way of civil works or controls over dust, noise, etc, being located well away from any settlement.

4.4.3   Feasibility of new 'model' reprocessing plant

1.   Costs

In order to examine the economics of centralised processing in a little more detail we have postulated a new plant in what are considered to be fairly typical circumstances. The likely resulting costs and revenues are analysed in order to gain a broad understanding of the potential economic viability of such plants.

The main features of the plant would be:-

Capacity   - Design input of 216,000 tonnes/year mixed
                   demolition waste.
                   Output of 185,000 tonnes/year of fine aggregate,
                   coarse aggregate and steel scrap (2%).

Restrictions   - Maximum 1 metre diameter material.
                   High proportions of plaster, mortar or wood not
                   accepted.

Broad specifications and the cost basis of the plant are given in Table 4.4(b).

In Table 4.4(c) we have estimated total recovered material costs.

It will be seen that on the basis of the assumptions taken, which includes a relatively high rate of interest recovery, to allow for

Table 4.4(b)		
BROAD SPECIFICATIONS AND COST BASIS OF A HYPOTHETICAL PLANT TO PROCESS CA.185,000 TONNES OF DEMOLITION WASTES PER ANNUM		
Item	Description	Estimated or Assumed Cost Basis $
Site area in m^2	15,000	Annual rental of $2 per m^2
Average production rate in tonnes per hour	100	1 x 8 hour shift per day, 5 days per week, 46 weeks per year
Plant operating personnel	6	$20,000 per man year
Process equipment	- 2 x 50tph primary impact crushers, complete with feed equipment, grill and magnetic separator	$300,000 each
	- secondary cone or jaw crusher with screen	$200,000
	- 2 shovel loaders	$100,000 each
	- washer/dewatering plant	$50,000
	- compressor and pneumatic drill	$20,000
	- associated control equipment	$40,000
	- conveyors	$60,000
Civil and other works	Services available at site limits. Simple structure to enclose process plant, with dust extraction.	$70,000
Power consumption	400 MWh per annum	$75 per MWH
Maintenance	Labour and spares (Most costs for the crushers).	$0.40 per tonne = ca.$75,000 per annum
Other	Fuel, materials, etc. Disposal of residual matter.	$25,000 per annum $15,000 per annum

Table 4.4(c)	
CALCULATED PRODUCTION COSTS FOR THE HYPOTHETICAL PLANT	
Capital cost of plant (installed)	$ 1.3 million
Annual equivalent amortised at 25% over 15 years	337,000
Running costs per annum	265,000
Overhead costs per annum	90,000
Total annual operating cost	692,000
Average Production Cost per tonne of material recovered	3.74

a reasonable profit margin, production cost is calculated at $3.74 per tonne. Varying the capital cost by +50%, alters the processing cost by +$0.90/tonne, whereas reducing the interest rate to 12% would reduce the processing cost to $2.95/tonne.

2.   Revenue

Assuming 2% of the 185,000 tonnes a year of material recovered was scrap steel, and an ex-works price for scrap of $30/tonne, then a price of $3.20/tonne must be recovered for the recovered aggregate.

From Section 4.3.3, it was noted that the ex-works price for recovered aggregate in the U.K. was $1.90-2.20/tonne, whereas in Germany the ex-works Hamburg price for coarse and fine aggregates was approximately $4.00-11.00/tonne. If one assumes on an average ex-works natural aggregate price of $2.00/tonne, it can be seen that any processing plant situated close to a large conurbation is likely to be economic when that conurbation is situated more than 30-40 kilometres from the nearest natural aggregate sites. This assumes that the plant itself will be situated 10km from the market outlet, and that an incentive of $1.00/tonne will be required to persuade the construction industry to use recovered rather than natural aggregates.

3.   Conclusion

On a preliminary examination, it would appear that there is considerable scope for building and operating centralised demolition waste processing plants in situations where they would be economically viable. Nevertheless, for the following reasons, it should be realised that there is considerable uncertainty surrounding several aspects of this operation, namely:

- the types of processing and equipment needed to separate out concrete reinforcing steel and to produce aggregates of suitable quality;

- whether, in fact, recovered aggregates can be successfully used in new concrete production and other more critical applications.

However, the analysis served to indicate a number of important factors in relation to the economics of centralised recovery:

i.   Much will depend on centralised recovery plants being located close to the centres of major conurbations, both from the point of view of convenience and reduced transport costs for the demolition contractor, and to reduce the costs of delivering recovered scrap and aggregates to customers.

ii.   The ability of recovered aggregates to compete in terms of delivered price with natural aggregates is likely to depend considerably on the recovered aggregates enjoying a substantial net advantage over natural aggregates in respect of the costs of transporting the material to users.

iii. Circumstances where the prevailing level of costs for transporting and tipping demolition wastes is high could noticeably enhance the prospects for viable centralised recovery.

iv.   The way in which such plants are financed will have a significant effect on operating costs and thus on the potential for this form of recovery.

4.5   Indirect costs and benefits of demolition waste recovery and disposal

4.5.1   Environmental impact

The costs and benefits associated with the environmental impact of demolition waste handling, recovery and disposal are usually difficult to evaluate in quantitative terms.   A qualitative examination of the different environmental aspects is given in Section 6.

4.5.2   Import savings

There are two main reasons why the potential for import savings might give recovered products/materials an additional, unrecognised value.   These are the result of:

- potential benefits from an improved balance of payments;

- strategic gains from a reduced dependence on foreign materials.

With regard to the metals arising in demolition and construction wastes, the following proportions of the raw material (or its constituents), for which domestically recovered scrap metals may be substituted, are now imported into the EEC:

Pig iron (iron ore), steel scrap   -   70-75%
Aluminium as bauxite   -   29%
Lead as ore   -   54%
Copper as ore   -   68%
Zinc as ore   -   62%

With regard to energy, ca.59% of EEC primary energy suppplies are currently imported. It may be seen that imported metals and energy are of considerable importance as a feedstock in the EEC, with perhaps the exception of aluminium, so that there are strategic gains from metals recovery over and above the recognised value of the scrap.

A very high proportion of the other materials commonly used in construction are domestically produced, so that any social gains from raw materials saving through recovery are probably negligible. Energy consumed in producing natural mineral raw materials for construction is mainly for their transport. In some instances, recovery may lead to a reduction in materials transport, but recovery also involves the use of energy for processing, so that there is probably little, if any, net gain in the amount of energy consumed as a result of recovery. For items salvaged for re-use, however, the potential net gain in terms of energy consumption could be quite high, and so would result in some further savings on energy imports.

Recovery of non-ferrous metals undoubtedly provides considerable strategic and foreign exchange advantages to the Community. The total quantity recovered is not known, although it is unlikely that there is much scope for further increasing this figure. For steel, 1.8 million tonnes per year are recovered from demolition, and a further 230,000 tonnes could be reclaimed if reinforcing steel were to be reclaimed. Overall in the Community, this would reduce the marginal quantity of steel manufactured from imported iron ore and coking coal. For timber also, current re-use saves approximately 400,000 tonnes per year out of total arisings of approximately 2 million tonnes per year. With the introduction of new technologies for processing timber wastes into a re-usable form, or in by-product generation, there is obviously considerable scope for increasing this figure.

Finally, although currently little re-use of bricks, manufacture of concrete from reclaimed material, or production of aggregate from processed mixed rubble takes place, the increased recovery of demolition wastes would reduce overall energy consumption within the Community, backing out imports of oil and some coal. Very approximately, if 5% of mixed rubble were reprocessed, it is estimated that the total energy savings would amount to approximately 0.1 million tonnes oil equivalent.

Estimates of the overall balance of payments savings from recovery of materials in demolition wastes are shown in Table 4.5(a).

Table 4.5(a)		
CURRENT AND FUTURE POTENTIAL IMPORT SAVINGS FROM DEMOLITION WASTE RECOVERY		
$ million (1978 prices)	1978 Actual	Annual Potential 1985/90
Non ferrous metals	x	x
Ferrous metals (1)	135	280
Timber	460	920 (2)
Net energy (cement, brick, aggregate)	1	15 (3)
Total	596+x	1215+x

(1) Iron ore and coking coal equivalent to hot metal substituted.
(2) Assumes 40% recovery.
(3) Assumes 5% recovery of demolition rubble of which 10% re-used as bricks, 15% is used for concrete manufacture and 75% is recovered as aggregate.

From the above table it can be seen that the potential balance of payments benefit from increased recovery of demolition wastes is approximately $0.6 billion.

5. The potential for further recovery

5.1   The obstacles to further recovery

In Section 4, we have discussed various economic influences that
affect reclamation, and we have noted that new ways of using
recovered materials need to be developed if further recovery is
not to be constrained by lack of demand.

There are however many other reasons why additional recovery is
unlikely to take place under existing conditions, even though
reclamation of a material by a particular route might appear
attractive. Some of these reasons are specific (such as time
constraints, technical and market difficulties) and some are of
a more general nature. The various obstacles to additional
recovery are discussed below.

5.1.1   Technical difficulties/economic considerations

These arise particularly where recovery involves high-grade
recycling or re-use, and the removal of contaminants. Once
preliminary sorting has been undertaken, demolition/construction
wastes normally arise in a highly mixed form. The proportion of
constituent materials in these wastes reflects the degree of
contamination present. Thus, since masonry and concrete invariably
comprise the major proportion of materials present in the waste,
one can consider these to be only lightly contaminated by other
materials. At the other extreme, extraction of the minute fraction
of glass or plastics from the waste causes considerable technical
problems due to the extremely high contamination by other materials.

Although there are technical solutions to the problems of separation and decontamination, for many materials the quantities
available for recovery are so small that the use of such processes
as cryogenic or eddy-current separation techniques (such as are
used in the secondary non-ferrous metals industry) is inhibited
by economic considerations.

The economics associated with available separation techniques
are likely to prevent recovery of all of the minor constituents
of mixed demolition waste, with the possible exception of timber.
Low-cost density separation, such as washer-dewaterer, has been
shown to be a viable stage in the recovery of materials from
demolition/construction wastes, both for the removal of soluble

sulphate from processed rubble, and for the stripping out of low density materials such as timber and plastics by flotation.

One particular technical obstacle to further recovery is associated with the separation of steel from reinforced concrete. Although it is possible to separate all of the concrete from its reinforcing using such methods as the wrecking-ball or pneumatic/hydraulic chisels, the time and energy requirement often exceeds the value of the recovered products especially when the reinforcing is in the form of a mesh. Studies of this problem have been undertaken recently both in Europe and in the United States, and promising techniques have been evaluated. These are discussed in Section 5.3.

5.1.2   The market for reclaimed materials

Even where the reclaimed material may have a considerable price advantage over the substitute raw material, there may still be limited demand for the reclaimed material due to:

i.   the actual or perceived quality of the recovered material;

ii.   the size of the market;

iii.   lack of information.

Quality of material. Standards for the use of secondary materials can be a major obstacle to materials reclamation. In some cases, there are clearly justified technical reasons for not using reclaimed material in new products. This applies for example, to prevent the use of demolition aggregate, containing a significant proportion of soluble sulphate, in new concrete manufacture.

However, in other cases, standards are less firmly based on the technical requirements, but may reflect more the qualities of the virgin material conventionally used than the real needs of the consumer. As an example, we have quoted in Section 2.4.3 a company that produces a heterogeneous, rough-sorted demolition rubble for use in road construction. User experience indicates this material to be highly acceptable as bulk-fill, whereas other road construction companies demand a much greater degree of homo-geneity, and essentially zero contamination in terms of gypsum, unfired clay, timber particles, etc.

A third situation can occur when the user perceives the product as inferior, even though its technical performance is similar to that of its virgin counterpart. For example, studies have indicated (31) that secondary concrete made from broken concrete aggregate can approach the strength of concrete made from natural aggregate when it is enriched with gravel at the expense of mortar.

Size of market. The market for products made with reclaimed material may be limited simply because there is only a certain overall demand for that type of product; for example, the amount of chip-board produced from waste timber that is wanted at any given time is dependent upon the overall pattern of consumption and production.

Fluctuations of overall demand in the economy have an impact
on the demand for secondary materials. At times when overall
demand is high, secondary materials are also in high demand
because of a general material scarcity. But often, during periods
of recession, demand for certain secondary materials is much
reduced. This is the recurrent problem facing the material recycling industry (32) and is most aptly illustrated in recent
years by wide variations in demand for scrap steel and waste paper.

The extent of the market for <u>by-products</u> tends to be a serious
obstacle to additional reclamation:

-   when there is a substantial quantity of the material,
    and the materials for which the secondary material
    substitutes are essentially low value and easily
    available. This applies to the use of concrete and
    masonry aggregate in road construction;

-   when alternative secondary materials are in competition.
    Again, in road construction, the availability of PFA and
    mining residuals can preclude the use of demolition
    rubble.

<u>Requirement for information</u>. Lack of information on the availa-
bility of wastes, or on their suitability for use in by-product
generation, can limit demand for reclaimed material. Some aid
in notifying possible users of waste arisings is now given in
many areas of Europe through "Waste Exchanges" (e.g. "bourse des
déchets industriels",recently introduced by the Chamber of
Commerce and Industry in Paris). In addition, "hardcore agencies"
exist in the United Kingdom, which specialise in introducing
potential purchasers of demolition or construction rubble to the
waste producer.

5.1.3   <u>The influence of time-penalty clauses in demolition contracts</u>

We have emphasised in Section 2.4.3 that the existence of a
time-penalty clause in a demolition contract can prove to be a
serious obstacle to materials reclamation. Such clauses are most
often included in the contract when the structure to be demolished
is situated in a high land-value area, such as an inner city area.
Stripping out, and salvage of materials is far less likely to
occur in such areas than in rural areas where the time factor is
not so important.

5.1.4   <u>Transport considerations</u>

In Section 4 we have commented upon the effects of transport costs
on the total cost of recovery of particular materials. Transport
costs can become a serious obstacle to recovery when:

-   the margin between product value and recovery costs is
    small. This is often the case for processed concrete
    and masonry rubble, although local factors, such as the
    delivered cost of natural aggregate, can greatly affect
    the value of the secondary product;

-       the distance between locations of arising, processing or
        storage site, and the secondary material user increase
        the total cost of recovery to above the value of the
        material to the user. This can particularly affect bulky,
        low density materials such as timber, when maximum vehicle
        payloads cannot be achieved.

5.1.5   Organisational obstacles

        In addition to the above specific obstacles to further recovery
        of individual materials, there are other ways in which the
        institutional framework may in practice inhibit additional reclama-
        tion. They relate primarily to the need for additional coopera-
        tion and/or new types of activity by existing organisations if
        additional reclamation is to be successfully carried out.

        We believe that the following represent the most significant of
        these obstacles.

        First, the quantity and quality of demolition and construction
        waste arisings, the potential value of particular constituents
        of the waste, and the means and costs of final disposal are all
        highly location-specific. Responsibility for handling the wastes
        can pass from the demolition/construction company to an independent
        transport contractor, and then to a local authority or private
        disposal contractor. Additional reclamation may well require an
        unaccustomed degree of co-operation between these organisations,
        together with a requirement for increased information concerning
        the potential value and demand of recovered materials in the
        locality.

        Secondly, some of the newer separation and upgrading technologies
        require a considerable input of capital. There are very few
        demolition companies in the Community that could finance such
        plant alone. This may require joint ventures between private
        companies and/or waste disposal authorities to establish well-
        equipped recovery plant.

        Finally, the central processing and recovery system that was
        envisaged in Section 4.4 requires a large throughput of waste
        if it is to be attractive in terms of recognised costs and values.
        This may require a greater degree of co-operation between waste
        producers, waste handlers and waste disposal authorities than
        is usual at present.

5.2   Technological changes affecting buildings and recovery potential

        Since the beginning of this century, there have been significant
        changes in construction materials and methods, changes which
        are posing particular problems to the demolition industry both
        in terms of the actual demolition process, and for the disposal
        of the resultant debris.

        As the proportion of 'modern' buildings requiring demolition
        increases, the effects of these technological changes will pose
        increasing problems to the industry, and furthermore, will affect

74

recovery potential due to changes in composition of the resulting waste stream.

Particular materials which have replaced, or are substituting traditional building materials include:

<u>Plain and Reinforced Concrete</u>	These products have largely replaced traditional materials both in structural uses (masonry, steel, timber) and in non-structural uses (roofing tiles, floors and pipework);
<u>Aluminium</u>	Aluminium products are beginning to replace items traditionally made of wood, such as doors and window-frames;
<u>Plastic</u>	Plastics are now used extensively, particularly for the manufacture of pipes, and fittings such as baths, sinks and flooring;
<u>Plate-glass</u>	This is now used much more extensively, as improved understanding of structural forces has enabled architects to allow greater proportions of the building's surface to be accessible to light.

There is no reason to believe that these trends in the use of materials are likely to change in the foreseeable future.

5.2.1   The effect of technological changes on demolition

All of the demolition contractors interviewed expressed considerable concern at their lack of readiness for coping with new (to them) types of construction. In particular, concern was expressed about the means of demolition of two commonly used construction techniques:

-       reinforced concrete structures;

-       buildings and structures containing pre-stressed or post-tensioned concrete members.

There are two major problems common to both of these types of structure. Firstly, construction drawings are very rarely obtainable for the building or structure when it is to be demolished. It can often be difficult for the demolition contractor to distinguish between construction methods, and the optimum demolition method to use may thus be difficult to select. This can lead to potentially dangerous situations, particularly in structures containing post-tensioned members, where the forces inherent in the highly tensioned tendon can cause sudden failure of the beam if load is removed by demolition. A trial and error approach to find the right method of demolition can be dangerous and also increases the cost of demolition.

Secondly, after demolition of such structures, handling and disposal problems are often encountered. Reinforced concrete beams arise after demolition as large and heavy masses. It is rarely considered economic by conctractors today to attempt to salvage steel reinforcing as the cost of energy required for separation often exceeds the value of materials. This is only likely to be achieved by increased economies of scale gained through processing the waste through larger plant (see Section 4.4). The beams must therefore be loaded onto vehicles for transport to disposal sites. Because of their mass, cranes are required to handle them. Plant, machinery and transport maintenance costs increase due to the difficulty of handling. Finally, the deposition of such large masses in tips causes further handling problems, and creates unstable conditions due to voidage.

5.2.2   The effect of technological changes on recovery potential

The four materials identified earlier will, to a varying extent, increasingly alter the composition of the Community's demolition waste stream. There will be a corresponding change in the potential for recovery of particular materials. This is discussed for each material as follows.

1.   Plain and reinforced concrete

As the proportion of reinforced concrete in the waste increases, there will be an increased potential for salvage of the steel reinforcing. The increased quantities will also provide a greater likelihood of the necessary economies of scale in reclamation to be achieved. The scope for processing concrete wastes separate from other demolition/construction wastes will also be enhanced.

Technologies are available for the separation of steel from reinforced concrete, and these are discussed more fully in Section 5.3. As more reinforced concrete structures arise in the waste stream, the economic incentive for introducing these technologies will improve.

We have not envisaged separate processing of concrete in our hypothetical system outlined in Section 4.4. However, if sufficient material is made available free of contamination from other constituents of the waste stream, a relatively pure concrete aggregate could be produced which could well command a higher price, or be suitable for a wider range of applications than an aggregate produced from mixed demolition waste.

2.   Aluminium

The production of aluminium products for use in building and construction has increased markedly in recent years, mainly due to its replacement of timber in the manufacture of window-frames and doors.

Our estimates of aluminium arisings in demolition wastes shown in Figure 3.9(c) indicate that increasingly significant quantities of used aluminium products will be found in these wastes. Any aluminium which is presently encountered by demolition contractors is salvaged, and sold to a specialist metals merchant for recycling. This situation is not expected to change.

Aluminium is a relatively high value material, and although recently there has been a fall in the real price of the metal because of the 1974/76 economic recession, it is unlikely that its real value will decrease over the long term.

3.   Plastics

Although it is generally accepted that the use of plastics in construction will continue to grow, there are few opportunities for resource recovery from plastics waste products that arise from demolition or construction activity. The main factors that combine to inhibit plastics recovery from these wastes are:

-        the low concentration of plastic materials in the waste;

-        the low value of the primary product;

-        the high transport costs that would be associated with transport of small quantities of low-density recovered plastics.

The only significant potential for recovery of plastic products from demolition activity is the stripping out of potentially re-saleable items such as bathroom fittings, and possibly flooring, prior to demolition.

4.   Glass

As with plastics, the potential for recovery of glass from demolition or construction wastes is negligible because of the small quantities that arise, the low value of the primary material, and because of the high degree of contamination by other materials in the waste.

Current reclamation of waste glass from demolition and construc-tion activities can be effectively considered as zero. The care necessary to remove and store window-frames together with their glass is uneconomic considering the low resale value. Removed flat-glass window-panes have no resale value on their own, as there is no uniformity of sizes. The only possible markets are as cullet in glass manufacture or for by-product generation, but the costs of separation, transport, cleaning and processing are inhibitive because of the way in which the waste occurs.

It is feasible that in two or three decades, some commercial buildings containing relatively large quantities of plate glass might require demolition. In such cases, there might be an economic incentive for removing the glass by hand prior to demolition.

5.3   The development of new end-uses

In the previous two sections, we have explained that the major obstacle to recovery of such items as glass, plastics and unrecovered non-ferrous materials is that the quantity of each material arising in the waste stream is very small, and its concentration is negligible. Separation and de-contamination costs therefore combine with transport and processing costs to inhibit recovery of these materials.

The three major recoverable constituents of the waste stream for which development of new end-uses can be envisaged are:

-        mixed demolition/construction rubble;

-        reinforced concrete masses;

-        timber.

Problems of recovery, and current and potential end-uses for each of these are discussed for the various materials below.

5.3.1   Mixed_demolition/construction_rubble

This material arises from the deliberate collapse of a building or structure, or from the excess waste material produced at a construction site after burial and site levelling. It therefore arises as an extremely heterogeneous mix containing pieces of masonry and concrete, earth, stones, gypsum and plaster products, timber, tiles, glass, plastics and very small quantities of metals.

The proportion of each material in the rubble varies according to the type of work, but as discussed previously, masonry and concrete constitute the major proportion of the materials.

Once separation has taken place, this decontaminated rubble may be size-reduced for application in the following end-uses:

i.   as bulk-fill in road construction;

ii.   as a base for tennis courts, parkland, etc.;

iii.   as a base around underground pipework;

iv.   as sub-base material in road construction;

v.   for new low grade concrete manufacture.

Such pulverised rubble is already used in certain parts of the Community in applications i, ii and iii, where the degree of contamination of the product is not too important.

For applications iv and v, specifications for the product include uniformity of particle size, and reasonable homogeneity. These are attainable with current separation, crushing and sieving technology, but the associated increase in processing costs tends to inhibit their use. There are also particular problems associated with these two applications:

-        for application iv, the road constructor requires very large quantities of similar material. The sporadic nature of demolition/construction waste arisings means that there would rarely be sufficient material available

to meet the total demand for this application at a
given time and locality;

-        for application v, the lack of market demand (as discus-
         sed in Section 5.1.2) inhibits use.

Even so, the extent of the potential market is indicated by the
fact that around 500 million tonnes of sand and gravel is used
for concrete manufacture in the EEC (33).

5.3.2   Reinforced concrete

If large and bulky masses of reinforced concrete are separated
at source, and processed separately to other constituents of
the waste, potential for recovery is enhanced by:

-        increased recycling of ferrous scrap;

-        recovery of relatively pure concrete.

Contaminant-free concrete waste, adequately size-reduced, may
have potential markets for the following end-uses:

i.   general bulk-fill usage;

ii.   sub-base or surface material in road construction;

iii.   new concrete manufacture.

The particular end-use will depend mainly upon the quality of
the resulting concrete particles. For application i. above,
only minimal size reduction and quality control is required.
For applications ii. and iii. however, control of mean particle
size and distribution must be exercised.

Size-reduction of reinforced concrete masses is normally only
undertaken to the extent necessary to reduce transportation,
handling and disposal problems. A wrecking ball is most often
used for this purpose. Occasionally, when time permits and
when the ferrous content of the reinforced concrete is sufficiently valuable, the wrecking ball or pneumatic/hydraulic chisels
may be used to completely separate the reinforcing from the
concrete. Such recovery, however, is rare, as the cost of time
and energy required often exceeds the value of ferrous material
recovered.

New techniques for the separation of steel from reinforced
concrete require development; techniques which preferably will
also pulverise the concrete into a form in which it may be used
in applications ii. and iii. above.

The 'Centre Scientifique et Technique de la Construction' (CSTC)
in Belgium is examining the practicality, and economics, of
using explosives to fragment large reinforced concrete masses
to a very fine mean particle size, leaving the steel reinforcing
available for recycling, and concrete particles available for
re-use.

The CSTC is also investigating the claims of a French manufacturer of pulverising plant. The "Concasseur Brocas", it is claimed, will pulverise reinforced concrete structures at a rate of 25-30 tonnes per hour. The steel and concrete are completely separated, and the particle size of the concrete enables re-use in high grade applications such as given in ii. and iii. above.

The estimated costs of both these methods are given in Appendix 11, and it would appear that both have the potential for economic application.

Both of these studies are being undertaken as part of the "Three Countries Project" (see Appendix 10).

The cavitating water-jet has been suggested as a possible technique for separating steel from reinforced concrete. We are unable to comment on this technique as we have no knowledge of its use for concrete disruption in Europe. Some details of this process, also, are given in Appendix 11.

5.3.3   <u>Timber</u>

Current resource recovery from the timber fraction of the Community's demolition/construction waste stream is gained primarily by <u>re-use</u> of timber that is stripped out of buildings prior to demolition, or reclaimed from construction off-cuts.

In Germany, legislation that inhibits the tipping of timber wastes at landfill sites, and that prevents the burning of timber on open fires, promotes <u>by-product generation</u>, principally as heat recovery at incineration plant. However, costs associated with incineration are high (see Section 4.2.5).

Re-use, or by-product generation from demolition timber waste, involves the handling of a raw material which may contain nails or other contrary matter, may have been chemically treated, may be painted and/or infected, and may be made up of a variety of types and sizes. These characteristics pose considerable technical problems for processing and quality control, and even where they can be overcome, there must be considerable doubt about the economic attractiveness of such processes.

However, current and potential end-uses for reclaimed demolition and construction timbers include:

i.   direct re-use (doors, floorboards and the like);

ii.   re-use with minor processing (requires de-nailing and/or sizing);

iii.   the production of particle- or chip-board;

iv.   the production of pulp for the paper industry;

v.   energy recovery.

Currently, only the first two markets provide significant outlets for demolition timber waste. Even so, re-use with minor processing could be further enhanced through improved techniques such as the use of the cavitating water-jet (see Appendix 11), which is claimed to be capable of cutting timber economically. Such techniques solve problems associated with the cutting of nail infested timbers. There is no shortage of markets for timber in re-usable form; nor do we envisage that this situation is likely to change in the future.

As far as we know, there is no commercial production of chipboard from demolition waste timber. However, there are pilot plants for producing chipboard from this source material, one in Berlin, the other in Los Angeles. The plant in Los Angeles uses a hammermill, and it is stated that nails have not been a major concern. The Berlin plant specifies reasonably clean timbers with negligible contamination from other materials, and a low degree of nail infestation.

The more demanding uses of demolition waste timber, such as feedstock for producing pulp, have serious practical difficulties associated with them in view of the nature of the waste.

As an overall point concerning the re-use of contaminated and broken timber, it should be recognised that it is significantly more expensive to transport as a separated material than other demolition materials.

For chemical or thermal conversion such as acid hydrolysis or pyrolysis, research and operating experience in connection with the treatment and recovery of municipal and other solid wastes, does not suggest any significant potential for converting demolition waste timber. These processes are costly to build and to operate, and available evidence indicates substantial economies of scale will be required before unit costs begin to compare and compete with more conventional forms of waste treatment. One refuse pyrolysis plant is operating at demonstration scale in Luxembourg, and another is being built in Frankfurt, Germany. In Canada, prototype plant for the pyrolysis of lumber wastes are being evaluated(34), and in the United Kingdom, a range of plant for the pyrolysis of such wastes has recently been marketed (35). In our experience, however, pyrolysis is unlikely to offer the contractor much advantage in terms of disposal charges compared with conventional incinerators.

From the point of view of the future economics of timber recovery from demolition waste, the expected future supply of hard and soft woods (36) relative to demand is such as to expect that the price of wood in its various forms will rise in real terms.

5.4   Action required to overcome the constraints to further recovery

5.4.1   Introduction

The obstacles to further recovery may be grouped into four broad categories: technical, market-related, organisational and external

economic factors. The following section will review the scope
and justification for reducing the constraints for additional
recovery of demolition waste materials, and identify those which
represent the priority areas.

Certain overall points can be made.

First, it is generally true to say that further recovery is more
constrained by the availability of market outlets than factors
limiting the separation and supply of secondary materials at
demolition sites. There is, of course, some inter-relationship
between the two, but this conclusion would argue that priority
attention should be given to increasing the market outlets for
materials than to improved recovery methods.

Secondly, while the scope for additional waste materials recovery
may well be significant if certain obstacles were removed, the
practical ability to alter the situation through government action
might be limited. This aspect will be discussed in the following
sections, and the Recommendations in Section 7 will take into
account the practical potential as well as the benefit of action
to be taken.

Thirdly, while in theory it is possible to influence external
economic factors affecting the recovery of secondary materials,
in practice such action could have wider implications which will
be unacceptable to the building industry, or administratively
difficult to put into effect. Nevertheless, the importance of
these factors should be recognised and the type of action necessary
to bring them about should not be lost sight of.

5.4.2   Market factors

Changes that are needed to increase the size and type of market
outlets can be summarised as follows:

- Improved dissemination of information on technical capa-
  bility on recovered materials, and on availability and
  origin of waste materials arisings. The setting up of
  regional Waste Material Exchanges and Agencies would
  provide the best means of achieving this objective.

- Redefinition of standards where unnecessarily high
  standards for the performance required are precluding
  use of recovered materials. In some cases, the establishment of standards of recovered materials, through testing,
  would indicate their suitability, where this is not
  widely known or accepted.

- More research into the suitability of secondary materials
  would also help to establish, in the users' opinion,
  whether or not recovered materials were effective sub-
  stitutes. Some research organisations, e.g. the CSTC
  in Belgium, the SVA and TNO in the Netherlands, and the
  BRE in the U.K. are already undertaking some work in this
  area.

- Provision and financing of centralised stock holdings
  would help to smooth out the fluctuations in supply and
  demand and contribute to the stabilisation of secondary
  material prices.

5.4.3   Organisational factors

The principal changes that would enhance recovery of waste
materials are:

- The establishment of larger and more integrated demolition
  contractors/joint ventures would improve co-operation and
  should reduce unit costs between the demolition, transport,
  disposal and recovery phases of the operation. This
  development would also enhance the ability of the industry
  to finance new plant and project development.

- The establishment of large centralised waste processing
  and recovery plants will be necessary to recovery and
  transport costs so as to provide sufficiently attractive
  commercial returns for expanded recovery of demolition
  materials.

- More co-operation between local authorities and demolition
  and disposals contractors could be achieved if time penalty
  clauses were more liberal, financial risks were reduced
  through the establishment of more stable secondary
  materials market,and better planning in approving the
  demolition of buildings, etc.

- Stricter control over tipping of certain waste materials,
  and of unlicensed tipping in general, would force other
  solutions to be found which should enhance co-operation
  within the industry and between contractors and local
  authorities and also help to advance the possibility of
  further secondary recovery.

5.4.4   Technical factors

Although first priority should be given to research into the
suitability of certain secondary materials in different building
applications, there is also a need for further R and D work in
developing improved construction, demolition and recovery techniques. Priority areas for work are:

- steel recovery from reinforcing concrete;

- demountable construction;

- timber cutting techniques;

- chipboard manufacture from recovered/contaminated timber.

It is not so much pure research that is needed in many of these
areas, but the testing of processes in pilot plants so as to
assess their technical and economic feasibility on a commercial
scale.

83

5.4.5   Economic factors

Improvement in the economics of demolition material recovery
could be achieved in a number of ways through intervention by
government:

i.   taxing of primary raw materials, e.g. aggregates;

ii.   subsidies on recovered materials;

iii.   fiscal incentives for use of recovered materials;

iv.   fiscal assistance and/or capital grants provided for the
         construction of secondary materials processing/recovery
         plant;

v.   taxes/higher local authority charges on dumping of
         demolition materials as landfill.

Many of the actions would have serious and perhaps unacceptable
wider economic implications for the construction as well as the
demolition industries. Options ii., iii. and iv. present potentially the most beneficial and administratively acceptable
courses of action, and therefore deserve more careful consideration.

5.4.6   Role of public authorities

It can be seen from this last section that there is a potentially
significant role to be played by government authorities in
reducing many of the existing constraints to further recovery
of secondary materials. Such action would need to be at local,
regional and national authority level, as well as public bodies
such as research institutions. Section 7, which sets out
recommendations for action, will refer to the type of government
body which is considered most appropriate to take particular
action in this area. Appendix 8 gives information on the
authorities that are responsible for demolition, use of materials
and disposal in each country, and also relevent details on
research organisations

6. Environmental problems and considerations

Environmental impairment can occur at any stage of demolition activity; by the actual process of demolition, transport of wastes, disposal and by resource recovery. The effect of further recovery potential on environmental impact at each of these stages is discussed below.

6.1 Demolition

The actual process of demolition must, of necessity, impinge upon the environment to some extent. The most common environmental complaints from such undertakings are noise, dust, vibration and the interruption of traffic or pedestrian flow. In addition, malpractice can cause further problems such as the danger of flying debris, or air pollution from the combustion of timbers on open fires.

Table 6.1(a) overleaf summarises ways in which the environmental impact of demolition work might be reduced, and also considers problems that may arise due to the introduction of such changes.

6.2 Transport of wastes

The transport of demolition or construction waste has the same effects on the environment as does road-haulage of any other material, i,e, directly observable effects such as exhaust air pollution, noise, vibration and the overcrowding and additional wear of roads. There are also indirect effects such as the depletion (or in part) of energy resources.

Increased recovery of demolition materials will have a significant beneficial effect upon transport-induced environmental impairment by:

-       reducing the quantity of material requiring disposal at distant tip-sites;

-       reducing the transport requirement for virgin materials.

Table 6.1 (a)

ENVIRONMENTAL IMPACT AND CONSIDERATIONS ASSOCIATED WITH DEMOLITION WORK

Impact	Means of Abatement	Comments
Noise	Hydraulic instead of pneumatic equipment. Exhaust silencers. Thermic boring.	High capital expenditure; negligible value of current equipment. Slight reduction in power; bulky. Health hazards in an industry reliant on transient, often untrained workers; atmospheric pollution; uneconomic for normal work.
Dust	Water-spray	Could be requirement for settling of run-off, if closures of gutters, drainage and conduits is to be avoided.
Atmospheric pollution from the combustion of timber, plastics etc. on open fires.	Legislative requirement for disposal by off-site incineration or landfill. (Timber combustion is already forbidden in many Member States, but only in Germany is this practice completely eliminated).	High cost of incineration; difficulty of disposal at landfill sites; few markets for re-use or resource recovery.
Disturbance to local environment (access, traffic flow, etc.	Reduced use of large plant (cranes, tracked vehicles etc.)	Costs of demolition will be significantly increased. Use of pneumatic chisels, thermic lances etc. will result in other impacts as detailed above.
Vibration	As above	As above
General malpractice	Enforceable code of practice for demolition.	Requirement for adequate inspectorate.

In particular, a substantial increase in local recovery concrete and/or brick rubble (to substitute for natural aggregates in low or high grade end-uses) may in many urban localities significantly reduce the number of vehicle movements required for virgin material haulage.

6.3   Disposal

Virtually all demolition and construction wastes that arise in the Community are disposed of at public or private tipping sites, or at other land-fill areas. Very often their effect may be beneficial, as when they are used in land reclamation schemes, or as covering material in mixed-waste tips. At other times, and in particular localities, disposal of these wastes can prove detrimental to the environment:

-        in high land-value areas and where there is a shortage of available tipping space, there is an increasing requirement for wastes to be transported to far-distant landfill sites;

-        by uncontrolled disposal practice: privately owned excavations such as clay pits are often filled with these wastes. Whilst not posing any immediate threat to the environment, such practice diminishes space that might be suitable for more noxious wastes (municipal or industrial);

-        by illegal disposal practice: in areas where tipping availability is low, and charges high, problems are sometimes encountered due to owner-drivers disposing of wastes at any nearby construction, or other open site;

-        at the tip site: the disposal and subsequent degradation of timber, and voidage caused by large irregular masses of concrete and masonry, can create problems of instability at landfill sites.

Increased reclamation of demolition wastes will reduce the amount of material requiring disposal, and will thus lessen the environmental impact of the above factors.

6.4   Materials recovery

Increased recovery of demolition materials can be expected to have both beneficial and detrimental effects on the environment. Likely beneficial effects include:

-        a reduction in transport requirements;

-        conservation of landfill space;

-        savings in virgin or imported resources; the widespread use of demolition rubble as aggregate material would markedly reduce demand for the virgin material thus reducing environmental damage caused by extraction, processing and transport of the virgin material;

- savings in energy resources consumed in the production of ferrous and non-ferrous metals;

- a reduction in amenity destruction; lowered demand for virgin material extraction (mainly natural aggregate but also iron-ore and timber) would lessen requirement particularly for new quarrying operations.

There are however likely to be some detrimental effects upon the general environment associated with increased resource recovery from demolition materials, the most significant of which are:

- noise, dust and vibration: caused by size-reduction techniques for the processing of concrete and masonry rubble;

- air pollution increase: due to the incineration or other energy conversion of combustible fractions of the waste;

- requirement for effluent treatment: when water is used during recovery (e.g. dust control, separation by floatation);

- localised amenity destruction: the siting of a centralised processing plant will involve local amenity destruction due to the operations of the plant and to the high transport requirement;

- industrial dislocation: changes in the industrial structure might be required, such as some movement of labour and resources from extraction and production of virgin material towards the collection and treatment of wastes.

Overall, increased materials recovery must be seen as providing a means of significantly reducing the impact of the demolition industry. We conclude this to be the case even when the impacts of a centralised treatment plant of the type described in Section 4, situated near to an urban area, are taken into account. For it must be borne in mind that such plants are only likely to be justified when there is a shortage of local land-fill tips, and where natural aggregates have to be transported long distances.

Localised environmental disruption may be minimised by optimum siting, (away from habitated areas), civil engineering design, (to eliminate or reduce noise, dust, vibrations etc.) and optimal transport routing.

6.5   Asbestos

6.5.1   Introduction

The following account of asbestos use in the construction industry and its associated problems in demolition refers mainly to the situation in the U.K. Some information was obtained from other Community Member States, but not as comprehensive as that obtained from the U.K. While the problems

associated with asbestos use are assumed to be similar throughout the EEC, the steps being taken to control asbestos production and relevant legislation may vary from country to
country.

6.5.2   Uses of asbestos in construction

Of the 5 million tonnes of asbestos mined annually world-wide,
95% is chrysolite (white asbestos), the remainder being largely
crocidolite (blue asbestos) and amosite (43). The major
properties of asbestos which make it valuable in the construction industry are its tensile strength, heat and fire resistance, resistance to chemical and biological attack and its
relative low cost. This last advantage is however decreasing
due to the increasing cost of meeting asbestos dust-reducing
costs in the production process.

White asbestos is the most commonly used type in the construction industry and is found in cladding, roofing sheets, tiles,
asbestos cement cellulose products, sewerage pipes and as
filler and reinforcement.

Table 6.5(a)

ASBESTOS CONSUMPTION IN THE EEC

Country	Total Consumption (1000 tonnes)	Consumption by construction industry (1000 tonnes)	
		Total	For asbestos-cement products
Belgium and Luxembourg	87 (1973)	n/a	23 (1976)
Denmark	33 (1973)	n/a	
France	144 (1976)	n/a	87 (1976)
Germany	382 (1976)	n/a	102 (1976)
Ireland	7 (1973)	n/a	n/a
Italy	74 (1976)	n/a	n/a
Netherlands	49 (1976)	n/a	10 (1976)
United Kingdom	143 (1976)	100	51 (1976)
EEC	919	n/a	ca.280

Source: Roskill Report on Asbestos 1978 (45)

Table 6.5 (b)

ESTIMATED BREAKDOWN OF ASBESTOS FIBRE USAGE IN EEC COUNTRIES 1973/76

	Belgium & Luxembourg %	Denmark %	Ireland %	France %	Italy %	Netherlands %	United Kingdom %	West Germany %	TOTAL %
1. Asbestos-cement building products	54	78	67	40	58	29	32	47	45
2. Asbestos-cement pressure, sewage and drainage pipes	17	2	24	32	27	13	5	19	20
3. Fire-resistant insulation boards	6	9	9	1	-	-	13	0.2	4
4. Insulation products including spray	-	1	-	2	1	-	2	0.2	1
5. Jointings and packings	0.1	4	-	1	1	-	7	6	3
6. Friction materials	1	5	-	3	3	-	10	8	5
7. Textile products not included in (6)	1	-	-	3	3	-	5	3	3
8. Floor tiles and sheets	-	2	-	9	1	-	9	7	6
9. Moulded plastics and battery boxes	2	-	-	1	1	-	2	1	1
10. Fillers and reinforcements and products made thereof (felts, mill-board, paper, filter pads for wines and beers, underseals, mastics, adhesives, coatings, etc.)	19	-	-	9	5	58	15	8	12
TOTAL	100	101	100	101	100	100	100	99.4	100

Blue asbestos is used extensively in the manufacture of asbestos cement pressure pipes but these are no longer used in the U.K. A voluntary ban on import of blue asbestos products to the U.K. has been in force since 1970. Blue asbestos products are, however, found in many buildings constructed prior to 1970.

Asbestos fibre may also be sprayed onto surfaces and provides a range of properties from thermal insulation and fire protection to noise reduction and condensation control. In the U.K., prior to 1970, the application of sprayed asbestos to buildings was not subject to the Asbestos Industry Regulations of 1931 and blue asbestos was often included in the spray. The stringency of the levels of crocidolite dust permitted under the new Asbestos Regulations effectively bans the use of blue asbestos,and substitute materials and methods have generally taken over from asbestos spraying.

Amosite asbestos is used principally for the manufacture of insulating boards due to its superior heat resistant properties (44).

Some information on the quantities of asbestos used in EEC Member States is given in Tables 6.5(a) and 6.5(b).

6.5.3   Health hazards

The major health hazard associated with the production and handling of asbestos arises from the inhalation of asbestos fibres which causes gradual formation of scar tissue on the lungs (fibrous) and may lead to one or more of a number of diseases (43).

asbestosis - usually associated with occupational exposure;

cancer of the pleura - asbestos is the only known cause of this desease in humans; it may take up to 50 years to develop;

mesothelioma - relatively rare form of cancer which has been known to develop after short periods of exposure.

Concern over asbestos as a health hazard is generally concentrated on occupational exposure. Conditions in British asbestos factories are now the responsibility of the Health & Safety Executive, Factory Inspectorate. In the construction and demolition industries the Factory Inspectorate undertakes an advisory role and may be called on to carry out air sampling (46).

6.5.4   Regulations and legislation

United Kingdom

Standards for exposure to asbestos dust in the U.K. are laid down in the 'Asbestos Regulations, 1969' which apply whenever emission of dust is likely to arise from use or handling of asbestos materials (47). Workers may be exposed to up to 2 fibres/millilitre of air (0.2/ml for blue asbestos) throughout the working day. If levels above these are found, respiratory protection must be provided (48). Frequent air sampling should be carried out to determine dust levels. Maintenance of safety precautions is the responsibility of both the contractor and employer (49).

Threshold Limit Values for other EEC countries

The following TLVs are currently in force within other EEC countries:-

Belgium	2 F/ml all types except crocidolite which is 0.2 F/ml
Denmark	2 F/ml all types
W. Germany	2 F/ml all types reducing to 1 F/ml by July 1982
France	2 F/ml all types
Ireland	2 F/ml all types except crocidolite which is 0.2 F/ml
Italy	There is a National Contract for asbestos cement workers only setting a limit at 5 F/ml, but for all other applications the industry is working within the UK limits
Netherlands	2 F/ml for all types except crocidolite but exemptions can be obtained for crocidolite for economical and technical reasons (50).

6.5.5   Demolition involving asbestos products

Removal of both blue and white asbestos is a specialised task which should be carried out under strict safety precautions by trained personnel. Buildings due for demolition should be carefully surveyed for asbestos and the types present identified. This is not always simple since the asbestos may have changed colour and X-ray analysis may be necessary to determine whether blue asbestos is present (44).

A number of safety precautions must be met, particularly where blue asbestos is present. These include:-

i.   complete segregation of working area, e.g. screening by plastic sheeting;

ii.   if blue asbestos is present, notification of Factory Inspectorate 28 days before work begins;

iii.   protection of workers - protective clothing and respiratory equipment for work in confined areas or where concentractions of dust exceed the statutory limits;

iv.   wetting of asbestos should be carried out before removal;

v.   collection and disposal should be carried out by recognised contractors obeying strict safety regulations (see 6.5.6);

vi.   after removal, the contaminated area must be cleaned and the air sampled to ensure an acceptable level of de-contamination (44).

Table 6.5(c) below suggests typical levels of asbestos dust
levels which might be expected during certain demolition
processes (44).

Table 6.5(c)	
EXPECTED LEVELS OF ASBESTOS DUST DURING DEMOLITION	
Operation	Fibres/ML
With thorough soaking	1 - 5
With use of water sprays	5 - 40
Carried out dry	20

6.5.6   Disposal of asbestos waste

Asbestos fibres are indestructible and the main object of
disposal is to present their becoming airborne again. The
generally recommended method of disposal of asbestos waste
is packing in heavy duty polythene bags with burial as soon as
possible (47).

7. Conclusions and recommendations

7.1 Conclusions

The objectives of this study on demolition wastes can be summarised as follows:

- estimate the <u>quantities</u> of demolition and related wastes arising in the EEC and assess the different <u>types</u>;

- examine the current <u>uses</u> for materials/products recovered from these wastes, and estimate the present extent of recovery in member states, and review current and new means of waste handling and recovery;

- examine the <u>economics</u> of handling, recovering and disposing of these wastes;

- identify the scope for additional waste <u>recovery,</u> and the obstacles to achieving further re-use of materials, suggesting how these obstacles might be overcome;

- discuss the environmental implications of recovery of demolition wastes;

- make recommendations to the Commission on action that might be taken.

It will have been noted that there is a shortage of reliable data relating to waste arisings, recovery and disposal. The data presented should therefore be taken only as approximate indications of the quantities involved.

The following sub-sections describe the main points arising from the study.

7.1.1 Demolition and construction waste arisings in the EEC

We estimate that the amount of waste currently arising in the EEC from the <u>demolition</u> of structures is of the order of 80 million tonnes per annum, and that approximately another 80 million tonnes of waste arises annually from the construction of new structures, including associated earthworks, and the renovation and maintenance of existing structures. On a per capita basis, arisings would appear to be much higher in France, Germany, the Netherlands and the U.K. than elsewhere in the Community.

7.1.2   Sources of wastes and their composition

The overall amounts of waste arising in the EEC from demolition activity are composed mainly of:

Masonry   -   ca. 57% by weight

Concrete   -   ca. 37% by weight

Timber   -   ca. 2% by weight

The remaining 4% is made up of steel, gypsum and small amounts of non-ferrous metals, glass, ceramic matter, and plastics.

No detailed analysis of the quantitative significance of the different sources of waste can be made for the Community as a whole, as information for some member countries is not available. The amounts of waste generated by residential and non-residential building demolition and construction activity, civil works (roads, bridges, etc.), and hydraulic works (canals, harbours, etc.) vary substantially, both between member countries and regionally.

Most of the waste from construction is in the form of excavation material, which is largely made up of soil, rock, tree stumps, etc., and sometimes concrete where foundations are removed.

7.1.3   Future trends in quantities and composition

Forecasts of future demolition waste arisings were attempted on an input basis, by projecting the arisings of brick and concrete wastes using a number of simplifying assumptions. These materials already make up a high proportion of total wastes, and the proportion is expected to increase slowly. The forecasts indicated that, by the year 2000, demolition waste arisings in the EEC are likely to have doubled, and by 2020, tripled from present levels. Despite the tentative nature of our forecasts, it is clear that demolition waste arisings will continue to grow substantially. Concrete will become by far the most important constituent of demolition waste, largely at the expense of masonry and timber.

Forecasting on a similar basis, we estimate that the amount of ferrous metal arising from demolition will approximately triple from the present level of around 2 million tonnes per annum by the year 2000, and could increase five-fold on the present level by 2020. Significantly, the proportion of ferrous metals arising in the form of concrete reinforcing we estimate will increase from the present level of around 10% by weight of total ferrous arisings, to around 60% by the year 2000, staying roughly constant thereafter.

In addition, the amount of aluminium waste from demolition is expected to rise very dramatically in absolute terms, though it will still remain a relatively minor constituent of total demolition waste arisings.

No reliable basis exists for forecasting how quantities of wastes from construction, particularly excavation waste, may change in future but, in our view, these are also likely to increase considerably.

7.1.4   Current uses for materials recovered from these wastes and the degree of materials recovery

Demolition and construction rubble: of the total amount of masonry and concrete arising, approximately 20-25% is used for a specific purpose in the construction industry, either as base material in road building, embankments, etc., or as a surface in temporary roads and on mixed waste tips. This latter item forms a major outlet for rubble in the rainy season and can increase the total level of re-use to 50%. Except for a small amount (approximately 500,000 tonnes) of masonry and concrete in the U.K. processed for higher grade aggregate applications, this rubble is unprocessed. The re-use of unprocessed demolition rubble is very local and, as a result, the demand is normally very periodic. As will be discussed below, this is a major factor inhibiting further recovery of waste materials.

The remaining 75-80% of demolition rubble is disposed of as landfill and in land reclamation, much of which is uncontrolled.

Ferrous metals: a high proportion of ferrous metals in demolition waste, of which the majority is steel, is recovered - approximately 90%. Other than some re-use of rolled-steel joists and other constructional steel, these materials are sold as scrap. Most of the 10% that is not recovered is steel reinforcing, which cannot be easily separated from concrete.

All of the non-ferrous metals (copper, zinc, lead and aluminium) are recovered, except those which arise in small quantities and are highly contaminated, e.g. electrical wiring.

A certain amount of timber is currently reclaimed, either for direct re-sale (doors, window-frames, shelving, floorboards, etc.), or for use within the construction industry (e.g. as shoring material, fencing and shuttering). Estimates from contractors suggest that a maximum of 20% of total wood wastes from demolition are re-used, but recovery of these materials is again highly location-specific. There is currently no significant degree of by-product generation achieved through processing of timber wastes in the Community.

There is some recovery and re-use of bricks, stone-work and roofing tiles at certain locations, but reclamation of these materials on a Community basis can be considered as negligible.

Reclamation of other materials from these wastes (glass, plastics, ceramic tiles, bituminous waste from road reconstruction, etc.)

is negligible, chiefly because of their very low value, and also because they arise in only small quantities.

Principal economic factors

Price of natural aggregates: The delivered price of natural aggregates has a very significant effect on recovery of demolition and construction rubble, as the market for these recovered materials competes with natural aggregates. Only in urban conurbations, where a local scarcity of natural aggregates results in a high delivered price, is there potential for increased recovery by central processing plant which will produce a secondary aggregate. This potential is expected to increase in the long term as the demand for land forces virgin aggregate extraction further away from its markets.

Transport costs: The cost of transport is the most important factor affecting the overall level of recovery from demolition and construction waste. Road haulage is unlikely to be replaced by other forms of transport, and increased distance between the site of waste arisings, and the sites of processing plant or secondary user can eliminate any possible financial benefits to be gained from increased resource recovery. Transport costs are the basic influence affecting the price of natural aggregates, as considered above. Furthermore, for certain materials such as timber, their low density means that maximum vehicle payloads cannot be achieved, thus further increasing the costs of transport.

Scrap metal values: Recycling of metals in all cases offers significant savings in process energy requirements when compared with extraction from ore. Thus there is a strong likelihood that scrap metals will increase in real value in the long term, which would in particular be favourable to increased recovery of marginal types of material such as steel reinforcing.

Import savings: Finally, increased recovery of demolition/construction materials will provide some savings in imports, thereby contributing to an improved balance of payments, and reducing dependence on foreign materials. The most important materials which offer these gains are ferrous and non-ferrous metals, since, with the exception of aluminium, more than 50% of the raw material is imported into the Community.

For steel, 1.8 million tonnes per year are recovered from demolition, and a further 230,000 tonnes could be reclaimed if reinforcing steel were to be reclaimed. Overall in the Community, this would reduce the marginal quantity of steel manufactured from imported iron ore and coking coal. For timber also, current re-use saves approximately 400,000 tonnes per year out of total arisings of approximately 2 million tonnes per year. With the introduction of new technologies for processing timber waste into a re-useable form, or in by-product generation, there is obviously considerable scope for increasing this figure.

Finally, although currently little re-use of bricks, manufacture of concrete from reclaimed material, or production of aggregate from processed mixed rubble takes place, the increased recovery of demolition wastes would reduce overall energy consumption within the Community, backing out imports of oil and some coal. Very approximately, if 5% of mixed rubble were reprocessed, it is estimated that the total energy savings would amount to approx. 0.1 million tonnes oil equivalent.

The overall balance of payments benefit from recovery of demolition wastes can be summarised approximately as:

CURRENT AND FUTURE POTENTIAL IMPORT SAVINGS FROM DEMOLITION WASTE RECOVERY		
$ million (1978 prices)	1978 Actual	Annual Potential 1985/90
Non-ferrous metals	x	x
Ferrous metals (1)	135	280
Timber	460	920 (2)
Net energy (cement, brick, aggregate)	1	15(3)
TOTAL	596+x	1215+x

(1)   Iron ore and coking coal equivalent of hot metal substituted.
(2)   Assumes 40% recovery.
(3)   Assumes 5% recovery of demolition rubble of which 10% reused as bricks, 15% is used for concrete manufacture and 75% is recovered as aggregate.

From the above table it can be seen that the potential balance of payments benefit from increased recovery of demolition wastes is approximately $0.6 billion.

7.1.6   The potential for further recovery from these wastes, and the obstacles inhibiting additional recovery

Based on current estimates and forecasts of arisings, we have concluded that the materials which offer the greatest potential for additional reclamation are:

-        mixed demolition rubble;

-        uncontaminated concrete wastes;

-        timber;

-        steel from reinforced concrete.

The principal constraints preventing additional recovery of demolition waste materials can be summarised under the headings of:

-        market factors;

-       technical aspects of recovery;

-       organisational barriers;

-       external economic factors.

<u>Market factors</u>: The principal reason why more demolition materials are not re-used on a regular basis is the resistance of potential markets to the secondary materials, particularly if they are contaminated in certain respects. Some of this resistance is based upon <u>prejudice</u>, for example in the use of rubble in low base material in road construction, and in the re-use, in many areas, of bricks and construction timbers.

The other constraining factor is <u>inadequate knowledge of the suitability</u> of secondary materials in certain applications; for example the utilisation of processed concrete rubble in concrete manufacture, and the use of contaminated timber processed for chipboard manufacture or for paper pulp production.

The creation of <u>new outlets</u> for reclaimed materials will to a large extent depend upon the dissemination of information concerning the suitability of secondary materials, as well as research where there is inadequate knowledge in this respect.

<u>Technical aspects</u>: For certain materials, the development of new or improved technology will facilitate additional recovery. The most significant applications are:

-       development of improved processes for decontaminating mixed demolition rubble to produce a more homogeneous material suitable for higher grade applications;

-       a more economic method for removal of steel from reinforced concrete;

-       the development of cutting techniques for metal contaminated timbers;

-       the development of processes for manufacture of by-products from contaminated timber;

-       the development of mixed rubble pulverising plant.

<u>Organisational barriers</u>: The dislocation of the industry is such that demolition, transport, recovery and disposal operations of demolition and construction waste industry are usually the responsibility of different parties. Additional waste recovery will to some extent be dependent upon amalgamation or improved co-operation between the various contractors and local authorities. Co-operation can certainly be enhanced through improved dissemination of quantitative and qualitative information on the source and market outlets.

Secondly, the demolition contracting industry chiefly comprises of small companies unable on their own to finance the building and operation of large scale waste processing plant.

A greater degree of centralisation of waste processing, near to
the potential outlets, would provide economies of scale which
may be essential if additional steel and homogenous aggregate
is to be recovered. This is discussed earlier under Section 7.1.5.

External economic factors: The importance of the price of scrap
metal, aggregates and timber in influencing the economics of
materials recovery from demolition waste has already been discussed. In theory, taxes on these raw materials and/or subsidies
for reclaimed materials would stimulate the level of recovery.
In practice, such fiscal action by government may be considered
a case of the tail wagging the dog; this applies particularly to
taxing raw materials which would meet strong resistance from the
construction industry.

7.1.7   The disposal of demolition and construction wastes

When viewed in the context of the requirement for disposal of
household or toxic industrial wastes, demolition and construction
wastes are relatively inert and present few problems of disposal.

Construction wastes, comprised mainly of earthworks from site
excavation work, are often actively sought after either as covering
material in mixed waste tips or for landscaping purposes.

Demolition wastes tend to present problems of disposal only when
they are heavily contaminated with timber, plastics, metals or
large pieces of concrete. In particular, tip operators will often
refuse to accept waste which contains large quantities of timber.
In such cases incineration may be a solution, but the charges for
incineration are such that contractors wll tend to seek alternative means of disposal (e.g. burning on site).

Disposal charges are generally small, and may often be zero. This
applies particularly where land reclamation is underway, or cover/
fill material is required by the construction industry.

In certain areas of the Community however, disposal of even relatively
uncontaminated demolition rubble can present difficulties and be of
relatively high cost because of the high volumes of waste generated
coinciding with a local shortage of tipping space. Examples of such
areas are the densely populated regions in the South West of the
Netherlands, the Rhur area of Germany, and the Greater London
region of the United Kingdom. Particularly in such areas where
disposal costs are high, there are problems of uncontrolled and
illegal tipping of demolition waste (an exception to this is in
the Federal Republic of Germany, where legislative controls make
the waste producer responsible for the proper transport and disposal
of waste).

7.1.8   Environmental considerations

Both the demolition of buildings and the disposal of the waste
have considerable environmental impacts associated with them.
At the demolition and construction sites, disturbance, noise and
air pollution are the principal effects. There is little scope
for reducing these impacts even if the industry were to use
plant with more stringent noise and air emission control devices

and introduce new working practices. The cost of implementing such schemes are unlikely to be cost beneficial. The cost of enforcing such schemes by government would also be high.

The transport and disposal of rubble clearly also carry important environmental implications. These may be beneficial, such as the case of controlled tipping in certain areas where land reclamation is being undertaken. However, many high population areas of the Member States are increasingly facing a shortage of reasonably adjacent tipping sites so that long distance haulage is required. Also a considerable amount of uncontrolled and illegal tipping of demolition waste takes place. In such situations the handling and disposal of demolition wastes can be seen as having notable adverse environmental impacts. Additional recovery of materials can therefore be seen to provide a means for reducing the impacts, both of the transport and disposal of demolition wastes, and of the production and transport of substitute raw materials.

7.2   Recommendations

We set out below our recommendations for possible action with respect to the handling, disposal and reclamation of demolition and construction wastes in the Community. In developing these recommendations, we have taken into account the conclusions set out in the previous section.

7.2.1   Recommendations for action

i.   Demolition safety

The CEC should encourage the setting up of national registers to which the construction industry would submit records in the form of structural drawings which can be made available to demolition contractors. In particular, a register of buildings constructed with post-tensioned or pre-stressed structures should be compiled, and that this register should contain sufficient detail of each building for any special risks to be readily apparent to a structural engineer.

ii.   Harmonisation of legislation

We recommend that the CEC investigate ways by which individual national legislation relating to demolition practice and waste disposal may be harmonised. In particular, the adoption by all Member States of legislation that makes the waste producer responsible for the proper transport and disposal of the waste would be of particular benefit in reducing illegal disposal practice. This might best be achieved through demolition contractors having to submit records of the transport companies undertaking waste removal from sites.

In certain cases, legislative controls could directly contribute to improved recovery of secondary materials as, for example, in the Federal Republic of Germany where dumping of timber is prohibited.

iii.   Standards and specifications

The CEC should examine whether standards and specifications for
construction materials exclude the use of secondary materials
even where such secondary materials would prove technically
suitable. We recommend that national bodies responsible for
building and construction materials specifications should be
asked to co-operate in laying down specifications for reclaimed
materials and products, and the categories of uses to which
secondary materials and products of these specifications could
be put. These categories should conform with any raw material
categories. This action could have particular relevance to the
increased use of crushed bricks and concrete wastes in road
construction and in new concrete manufacture.

iv.   Publicity about standards and specifications

The CEC should encourage the relevant authorities to prepare a
programme of publicity to inform the potential users of reclaimed
materials and products about the standards proposed in R.iii and
the performance that can be expected as compared with the
comparable virgin material or product.

v.   Structural design

The CEC should examine how the construction industry could take
recoverability of materials into account when designing buildings
and structures. This is of particular relevance in the case of
pre-fabricated structural components, which might be designed
with suitable means of connection such that they could be dis-
mantled for re-use elsewhere, or for processing into raw material.
As this demountable construction is a relatively new concept,
encouragement could best take the form of research and development finance.

vi.   Collection of information

There is in many member states a lack of baseline information of
relevance to recovery. In particular, both quantitative and
qualitative data on demolition and construction waste arisings
either do not exist, or are based on extrapolations of data
from a particular locality or region. The estimates given in
this study should be considered for guidance purposes only. It
is therefore recommended that baseline studies should be made of
the waste arisings on a regional basis which could be disseminated to both secondary material users and relevant government
authorities and agencies. This is of particular relevance to
areas which might be considered for the establishment of central
processing plant. (see x. below).

It would be necessary to examine how data might most easily be
submitted, in what form the data might be most convenient to potential users and to co-ordinate the two; to examine the feasibility
of setting up data banks and the most appropriate institutions
through which the collection and data might be disseminated, and
to the number that might be required. Some assessment of the
cost/benefits of this exercise would need to be made.

vii.   Collection and dissemination of information on the
        technology and economics of secondary material recovery

To encourage further recovery of secondary materials, demolition
and disposal contractors, and local authorities should be better
informed on the latest techniques available for recovery and
processing of demolition waste materials, and the economics of
such processes. Efforts to increase awareness of the economic
and marketing benefits to be bestowed by centralised, large scale
processing plants should also be made. It is recommended that
the CEC should examine the most suitable means by which this
data collection and dissemination could be achieved, possibly
in conjunction with studies on the feasibility of setting up
regionalised data banks on waste arisings (see vi.).

viii.   Information for municipal authorities

We recommend that the CEC should take action to ensure that local
municipal authorities are aware of the options, economics and benefits for reclamation. In particular, we recommend that the
local authorities are made aware of the disadvantages of un-
necessary, or excessively strict time penalty clauses with
respect to demolition. We further recommend that the local
authorities should be given information on methods of co-operating
with waste producers, waste handlers and potential purchasers
of secondary materials - including the preparation of long term
contracts and be encouraged to establish joint ventures for
central demolition waste processing plant (see x. below).

ix.   Research and development finance

The CEC should give consideration to the support of demolition
waste material recovery through financed research and development. Such activity could be co-ordinated through the
European Communities Scientific and Technical Research Sub-
Committee on Raw Materials.

The scope for R&D financial support covers the following:

-       research on separation, upgrading techniques and uses
        for secondary materials, in particular:

        -       the recovery of steel reinforcing from concrete,
        -       size reduction and decontamination of timber,
        -       the re-use of structural components,
        -       the separation of secondary materials through
                demountable construction,
        -       less energy intensive methods for the size reduc-
                tion of demolition rubble;

-       research on the use of secondary materials and their
        products, in particular:

        -       new end-uses for aggregates made from mixed
                rubble,
        -       the potential for utilisation of concrete rubble

in new concrete manufacture and other high grade
uses,
- the use of demolition timber by-products in chip-
board manufacture;

- support of pilot plant construction and operation in the
above fields.

x.   Financial aid for central processing plant

In view of the potential importance of such plant in facilitating
the economic recovery of demolition waste materials and their
marketing, and also taking into consideration their high capital
costs, and the small size of the majority of demolition companies,
we recommend that the CEC should examine ways of providing
financial assistance to feasibility studies and subsequent pilot
plant development and operation for a central processing plant.

In order to help overcome the problem of fluctuating demand for
certain recovered demolition waste materials, feasibility studies
of central processing plants would need to assess how and to
what extent aid (in the form of grants or loans) might need to be
made available to finance the build-up of stocks.

xi.   Subsidisation of recovered materials

We do not feel a satisfactory case can be made out for discrimi-
natory taxation of raw materials to stimulate the recovery of
demolition wastes for re-use. However, we recommend that the
Commission should examine what level of subsidies might be
necessary to support a floor price for reclaimed aggregates
sufficient to render mixed rubble processing economically viable,
and to compare this with an evaluation of the social, environmental and economic benefits to be derived from reduced impact
of the transport and disposal of this rubble.

Appendix 1.   Detailed information relating to the estimation of waste arisings from new construction by country

A.1.1   Belgium and Luxembourg

The Quad City Project (6) estimated the quantity of removed debris from different types of buildings. These figures are reproduced in Table A.1(a).

Table A.1(a)	
NEW CONSTRUCTION: WASTE DEBRIS PRODUCTION	
Type of structure	Debris removed (tonnes) (i)
1 family brick	15
2 family brick	20
6 family brick	30
Industrial building ($5660m^3$)	70
(i) Assumes 1.3 tonnes per m^3.	

National statistical data on the numbers of different types of residential and non-residential buildings completed in Belgium and in Luxembourg between 1972 and 1976 enabled the estimates contained in Table A.1(b) to be compiled.

A.1.2   Denmark

Although transport companies are able to estimate the quantities of excavation materials carried, they are unable to differentiate between the amount of materials used as bulk-fill (the greater proportion) and the amount disposed of at landfill sites (a much smaller quantity). We are therefore unable to offer an estimate of construction waste arisings.

Table A.1(b)

ESTIMATED WASTE ARISINGS FROM NEW CONSTRUCTION IN BELGIUM AND LUXEMBOURG

| Country | Year | Waste arisings from new construction (000 tonnes) | | |
		Residential	Non-residential	Total
Belgium (i)	1972	574	430	1004
	1973	644	424	1068
	1974	678	386	1064
	1975	841	385	1226
	1976	775	383	1158
Luxembourg (ii)	1974	40	N/A	40(iii)
	1975	38	N/A	38(iii)
	1976	39	N/A	39(iii)

(i)   Basic source: Institut Nationale de Logement.
(ii)   Basic source: STATEC
(iii)   Residential construction only

Table A.1(c)

WASTE ARISINGS FROM CONSTRUCTION AND DEMOLITION –
POPULATION EQUIVALENTS

Regional Authority	Population*	Annual Arisings	Population Equivalent
Unit	1,000's	1,000 tonnes per year	Tonnes per inhabitant per year
Nice	438	244-292	0.56-0.67
Lyons	1,153	520	0.45

*   Regional populations: 1968 census

A.1.3   France

Information of a quantitative nature was obtained from various
local and regional authorities. Two authorities in particular
were reasonably confident about the quantity of wastes from
construction and demolition arising in their regions. In each
of these two regions, Nice and Lyons, there is only one major
tipping site at which these wastes are accepted. The quantities
of waste taken to these tips is related to the population served
as shown in Table A.1(c)

If these figures are used to estimate total arisings in France,
then the total quantity of construction and demolition wastes taken
to landfill sites, based on quantity of wastes per head of population, are currently between 24 and 37 million tonnes per annum.

By subtraction of the estimated figure for demolition waste
arisings (see Appendix 2.3), we estimate arisings of construction
wastes in France in 1978 at between 14 and 27 million tonnes.

A.1.4   Federal Republic of Germany

By subtraction of demolition waste arisings from total arisings
(see Appendix A.2.4), it would appear that some 36 million tonnes
of construction wastes were removed in 1975 of which a very high
proportion would be made up of excavation wastes. It is known
that a substantial amount of excavation wastes is put to some
use (as a fill material, landscaping, etc.), so that the quantity
generated is likely to be significantly greater than the above
figure. However, in terms of material disposed of, 36 million
tones would seem to be the best possible estimate presently
available.

A.1.5   Ireland

Information concerning the number of dwellings completed in
Ireland is contained in reference (20). We have assumed the
factors given in the Quad City Study Report for the amount of
debris produced for removal per new dwelling unit (see Table
A.1(a)).

From these data, our estimate for current waste arisings from
new construction in Ireland is approximately 350,000 tonnes per
year.

A.1.6   Italy

We have been unable to obtain any estimates of the quantities of
construction waste arising in Italy, either from demolition and
excavation contractors, or from national and regional authorities.
The only estimates that we are able to put forward are based on
the data given in the study referenced in Section 3.3.2.
Table A.1(a) shows the amount of debris removed by cause of
construction of different structures. The data shown in this
table are for numbers of dwellings completed annually. New

housing in Italy currently favours multi-family apartment buildings but there is also a significant proportion of 1-family houses. We have assumed that 50% of dwellings are in 1-family houses and the remaining 50% in 6-family buildings.

From our discussions with various agencies and organisations, we believe that wastes originating from the construction of non-residential buildings and structures will be very much less than those arising from the residential sector and in the absence of relevant data we have not included these materials.

Statistical information on new construction was gained from reference (11).

We thus estimate that the amount of waste arising from new construction in Italy is approximately two million tonnes per year.

A.1.7   The Netherlands

From Appendix A.2.7, our estimate for construction wastes that require disposal in the Netherlands is approximately three million tonnes each year.

A.1.8   United Kingdom

From Table A.2(e), our estimate for construction wastes that require disposal in the U.K. is approximately 23 million tonnes each year.

Appendix 2. Detailed information relating to the estimation of demolition waste arisings by country

A.2.1   <u>Belgium and Luxembourg</u>

A.2.1.1   <u>Residential demolition</u>

Our estimates of demolition waste arisings from housing are based on the material quantities of the 'average dwelling unit' that is demolished. It is assumed that such a dwelling is a two-storey, linked, single-family house having two separate walls and two linked walls (i).

The weight of materials in such a dwelling is about 120 tonnes, of which approximately 75% is due to masonry and 15% to concrete. The remaining 10% is made up of gypsum and plaster (3%), roofing tiles (2%) and timber (4%). The volume of the dwelling, excluding roof-space, is approximately 300m^3 (ii). It is assumed that such a dwelling unit is also typical of the majority of residential demolitions in Luxembourg.

A.2.1.2   <u>Non-residential demolition</u>

We have based estimates of waste arisings from non-residential demolition in Belgium on statistical data on the volumes of such buildings. A conversion factor of 0.22 tonnes of demolition debris per cubic meter of building volume has been used in the calculation. This factor was derived from work carried out on this subject in Europe and elsewhere (6). It is interesting to note that if the conversion factor derived from this work for a single family brick-built house (0.5 tonnes/m^3) had been used to estimate waste arisings from residential demolition, the weight of debris from an 'average dwelling unit' would be 150 tonnes, which compares reasonably well with the figure of 120 tonnes derived above from INS data.

Information on the number of non-residential buildings demolished in Luxembourg is not available.

(i)   Basic source: Institut Nationale de Statistique (INS)

(ii)   Based on the findings of a study on the quality of housing in Belgium. Enquête sur la qualité de logement en Belge. Institut Nationale de Logement, 1921.

Table A.2(a)

ESTIMATED WASTE ARISINGS FROM DEMOLITION IN BELGIUM AND LUXEMBOURG

| | Year | Demolition waste arisings (OOO tonnes) | | |
		Residential	Non-residential	Total
	1970	595	365	960
	1971	440	302	742
Belgium (i)	1972	457	261	718
	1973	451	287	738
	1974	384	324	708
	1975	316	436	752
	Year	Residential	Non-residential	(iii) Total
	1974	11.4	N/A	11.4
Luxembourg (ii)	1975	8.2	N/A	8.2
	1976	9.1	N/A	9.1

Notes:

(i)   Basic sources: Institut Nationale de Statistique
                      Confederation Nationale de la Construction

(ii)   Basic source: STATEC

(iii)   Residential demolitions only.

Table A.2(a) contains our estimates of total demolition waste arisings in Belgium and Luxembourg.

A.2.2   Denmark

A.2.2.1   Residential demolition

31% of the nation's housing stock is situated in the small area around Copenhagen, and almost three-quarters of these dwellings are in apartment buildings, most of which were built before 1919 (37). Most housing demolition in Denmark relates to such buildings, and the major causes of recent demolition are the Slum Clearance Act and the Fire Security Law (8). The great majority of these demolitions have been in the Copenhagen area.

An analysis of materials arisings from such an apartment building has been undertaken by researchers of the Kunstakademiets Architektskole, and we have assumed these data to be typical of the 'average dwelling unit' demolished in recent years. The results of this analysis indicate that approximately 52 tonnes of brickwork and 6 tonnes of timber result from the demolition of each dwelling unit.

Statistics on residential demolitions in Denmark are incomplete. However, discussions with the Ministry of Housing and with the Grundejernes Saneringsselskab (Slum Clearance Agency) indicated that the annual demolition rate is approximately 1000 dwellings per year.

A.2.2.2   Non-residential demolition

No quantitative information is available on the numbers or types of non-residential buildings that have been, or are due to be demolished; nor is there any considered information available on the quantities of waste materials produced.

The only figures we are able to offer for waste material arisings from these sources are subjective estimates given during our discussions with interested agencies and organisations in Denmark. It was suggested that total quantities of waste materials from the demolition of commercial property would account for approximately 50,000 tonnes per year, and that this would be predominantly brick-work and timber, in similar proportions as for housing wastes.

Our estimates of total demolition waste arisings are thus as shown in Table A.2(b).

Table A.2(b)				
ESTIMATED WASTE ARISINGS FROM DEMOLITION IN DENMARK IN 1978 (i)				
Structure	Materials arising from housing demolition (tonnes)			
	Copenhagen area		Total Denmark	
	Brickwork	Timber	Brickwork	Timber
Housing	32,000	3,700	52,000	6,000
Commercial	27,700	3,000	45,000	5,000
TOTAL	59,700	6,700	97,000	11,000
(i) Excludes non-residential demolition waste other than wastes from demolition of commercial buildings.				

A.2.3   <u>France</u>

We have attempted to estimate demolition waste arisings by extrapolation of figures gained from demolition contractors. These figures themselves were little more than intelligent guesses, and must therefore be treated with caution.

We spoke with the five major demolition companies in the Paris region, most of whom employ between 35 and 50 staff. The figures obtained from these companies suggest that each worker accounts for about 2,000m^3* of waste material (as brick, concrete, stone and timber) annually and about 20 tonnes of steel.

The contractors' association, the "Federation des Entrepreneurs de Demolition" believes that in the Paris region, there are about 500-600 people working wholly in the demolition industry at the present time (compared with 900 two years ago). Subjective estimates suggest that these workers account for about half of the total work undertaken. We therefore estimate the quantity of material currently generated by demolition work in the Paris region to be approximately two million tonnes per year of waste material, and 20,000 tonnes of steel.

Given a population of 9.9 million inhabitants in the Paris region**, and a national population of 52.6 million, we can extrapolate the above figures for the whole of the country:

-       10.4 million tonnes per annum of waste material

-       104,000 tonnes per annum of ferrous metal

A.2.4   <u>Federal Republic of Germany</u>

The Federal German Government, in preparing its Waste Management Programme, 1975 (38), estimated the total quantity of demolition and excavation wastes <u>for removal</u> in 1975 at 5 million tonnes. More recently, the Federal Environment Agency (Umweltbundesamt) completed an analysis of information collected under the Environmental Statistics Law (7), which indicated total arisings of demolition and construction wastes, including excavation wastes, of some 72 million tonnes in 1975. The size of this estimate was a cause of some surprise within the Federal Environment Agency, so much so that the analysis is presently being checked for any mistakes. However, interviews carried out with the Deutscher Abbruch Verband and a number of demolition contractors, suggest that this estimate is not far wrong (a rough check was made by aggregating the approximate quantities of material being handled by DAV members).

Although the above analysis does not distinguish between demolition wastes and construction wastes, those representatives of the demolition industry contacted broadly agreed that around

---

*   1m^3 = 1.3 tonnes

**   Eurostat 1977

50% of the total quantity estimated by the Federal Government originates from demolition, i.e. circa 36 million tonnes of demolition wastes in 1975.

There are no data available on the <u>sources</u> of demolition wastes, i.e. the types of structure involved.

A.2.5   <u>Ireland</u>

A.2.5.1   <u>Residential demolition</u>

It is assumed that the average weight of materials arising from the demolition of one dwelling in Ireland is similar to the figure obtained in both the U.K. and in Belgium, i.e. 120 tonnes per dwelling (see Appendices A.2.1 and A.2.8).

Demolition waste arisings in Ireland are then estimated as the product of the average weight of materials per dwelling, and the number of dwellings demolished*, from which current arisings are approximately 40,000 tonnes per annum.

A.2.5.2   <u>Non-residential demolition</u>

We are unable to offer any estimates of waste arisings from non-residential undertakings as quantitative information concerning these sectors is not available. It would be unwise to attempt to relate the proportions arising from these sectors to information from the U.K., as the industrial base of the two countries is quite dissimilar.

A.2.6   <u>Italy</u>

We have estimated quantities of demolition wastes arising from the volumes of buildings demolished, utilising conversion factors (volume of debris generated per cubic meter of building volume) as given by demolition contractors. Approximately 18% of communes in Italy do not file statistical returns. Since these are mostly small rural communes that do not significantly affect the balance of the statistics that are of interest in this study, no allowance was made for this.

The following conversion factors were suggested to us during our discussions:

-     A conversion factor of 0.3 should be applied to total volumes of industrial and public buildings in order to obtain volumes of wastes arising. This applies to old brick-built factories, etc. When demolition starts to deal with reinforced concrete structures, this factor falls to 0.15.

-     A conversion factor of 0.4 applies to old, brick-built residential buildings.

---

*　Source: Building and Construction Division, DoE, Dublin.

In calculating the weight of demolition waste, we have assumed an overall density of 1 tonne/m^3 for the mixed rubble. This figure is somewhat less than the density normally used for masonry and concrete rubble (1.3 tonnes/m^3) as we have made allowance for the effect of timber, gypsum and plaster products, and other low-density materials present.

Statistical information on the age and volume of buildings at demolition is available for the non-residential sector, and we have assumed that such buildings built prior to 1925 were predominantly brick-built, and that those buildings built thereafter were constructed mainly in reinforced concrete.

All of the statistical information was obtained from reference (11).

Table A.2(c) contains our estimates of demolition waste arisings in Italy.

Table A.2(c)		
ESTIMATED WASTE ARISINGS FROM DEMOLITION IN ITALY		
Year	Demolition waste (OOO tonnes)		
	Residential	Non-residential	Total
1974	753	566	1319
1975	529	491	1020
1976	528	373	901
1977	474	267	741

A.2.7   The Netherlands

Several studies of both a quantitative and qualitative nature have already been undertaken in the Netherlands concerning arisings of demolition and construction waste.

The most commonly quoted study is that undertaken by the Stichting Verwijdering Afvalstoffen (SVA). In 1976, information was obtained from transport companies which suggested that the total quantity of construction and demolition waste transported to disposal sites was about 6.5 million tonnes during that year (39).

In 1977, the Central Bureau of Statistics (CBS) reported to the Ministry of the Environment on quantities of construction and demolition waste arisings (40). Measured data, again from the weight of material carried by road, gave a figure of 7.1 million tonnes excluding soil for 1976. CBS estimates indicated that a further 8.5 million tonnes of earthworks (soil, earth, stones, etc.) was also carried by road during that year.

116

Table A.2(d)

QUANTITATIVE ESTIMATES OF DEMOLITION AND CONSTRUCTION WASTE IN THE NETHERLANDS

Study	Year	Basis		Demolition and Construction Waste				Earthworks, soil, earth, stones '000 tonnes
		Waste arriving at tip	Material transported by road	Measured arisings '000 t	Population served '000	Population equivalent kg/inhabitant	Estimated national arisings '000 t	
S. Holland	1974	✓		1,960(i)	3,018	649	8,885	-
SVA	1975	✓		1,890(i)	2,800	676	9,240	-
SVA	1976	✓		6,500	13,670	475	6,500	-
CBS	1976		✓	7,100	13,670	519	7,100	8,500

Note: (i) Assumes 1.3 tonnes/m^3

117

Also in 1977, the Province of South Holland reported on a solid waste plan for the region, which included a sub-report on wastes from demolition and construction (41). In 1974, wastes arising at tipping sites in the region were monitored and the total wastes measured were related to the population served to give a per capita figure. It was found that during the year, each inhabitant in the area was responsible for the production of $0.5m^3$ of construction and demolition waste.

In 1975, another SVA study monitored the quantity of wastes arriving at tipping sites (9). The sites in question served the densely populated Amsterdam-Rotterdam-Delft-Den Haag area and the measured quantities of construction and demolition wastes were again related to the population served. A figure of $0.52m^3$ of construction and demolition waste per inhabitant was obtained.

Table A.2(d) summarises the above data, and current arisings of demolition and construction waste are thus approximately seven million tonnes per year.

It is not known what proportion of this figure is due to demolition activity. Table A.3(g) indicates that about 60% of this waste by weight is due to masonry, concrete, timber and mixed household waste, materials which are normally considered to be the main components of demolition waste. We therefore estimate that approximately four million tonnes of demolition waste require disposal each year and a further three million tonnes of construction waste also are taken to tipping sites.

A.2.8   United Kingdom

A.2.8.1   Total quantities

We have estimated arisings of demolition wastes from information obtained from local authorities relating to the quantity of demolition and construction wastes tipped in their areas.

Table A.2(e) contains the results of our discussions, and indicates that the total quantity of demolition waste that is disposed of at public or private tipping sites is approximately 20 million tonnes each year.

A.2.8.2   Residential demolition

Almost all housing that has been demolished in recent years was built prior to 1918(i). Most of these dwellings were of the one-family terrace type, constructed mainly in brick with timber frame. Subjective information gained from demolition contractors suggests that demolition of such housing will account for between 100-120 tonnes per dwelling, of which up to 20% is due to concrete, and nearly all of the remainder is due to brick or stone. A small percentage by weight (approximately 2½%) of timber will result, and 5-6% of fittings.

(i)   Source: Housing and Construction Statistics. DoE.

118

Table A.2(e)				
ESTIMATED TOTAL WASTE ARISINGS FROM DEMOLITION AND CONSTRUCTION				
Area	Population	Annual Waste Arisings (tonnes per inhabitant per year)		
	'000s	Demolition	Construction	Total soil and rubble
S. Yorkshire(i)	1317	0.332	0.405	0.737
E. Sussex	657	N/A	N/A	0.75
W. Sussex	623	N/A	N/A	0.63
GLC	7111	0.35	0.427	0.777
U.K.	55900	0.33-0.35	0.40-0.43	0.63-0.78

(i)   Source: Alternatives in Waste Disposal. South Yorkshire County. LGORU Report No.C212, 1975

Based on these figures, and a current demolition rate of approximately 50,000 dwellings per annum (i), we estimate total arisings from housing demolition to be approximately 5.5 million tonnes per annum.

A.2.8.3   Non-residential demolition

By difference, we estimate total waste arisings from the demolition of non-residential buildings and structures to be approximately 14.5 million tonnes per annum.

(i)   Source: Housing and Construction Statistics. DoE.

Appendix 3.   Detailed information relating to the estimation of the composition of demolition wastes in each country

A.3.1   <u>Belgium and Luxembourg</u>

The composition of wastes generated from housing demolition is estimated from the constituent materials of housing currently demolished. The information given in Appendix A.2.1 contains this data.

The composition of wastes arising from non-residential demolition is much more difficult to identify. Contractors normally under-take work in both the residential and non-residential sectors, and those interviewed were unable to offer any detailed informa-tion concerning the composition of wastes from either sector, other than to state that there is a significantly higher propor-tion of concrete waste from the non-residential sector.

We are aware of only one study that has been undertaken in the Community which differentiates between wastes arising from housing and demolition, and those which are generated by the demolition of non-residential structures. The Building Research Establish-ment in the U.K. has undertaken a postal survey of demolition contractors, and it was estimated that 29% of wastes from non-housing demolition was due to masonry, 36% to plain concrete, 21% to reinforced concrete and the remaining 14% was mostly comprised of steelwork (10). As construction methods and materials are broadly similar in most of the Member States - particularly for the non-residential sector - these figures are used in the absence of Belgian data to estimate the composition of wastes from non-residential demolition.

Our estimate of the composition of demolition and construction wastes in Belgium and Luxembourg is thus as shown in Table A.3(a).

A.3.2   <u>Denmark</u>

Appendix A.2.2 contains information relating to the materials composition of the typical dwelling unit that is demolished in Denmark. The only qualitative information available concerning the composition of wastes from non-residential demolition suggests that the 50,000 tonnes per year of wastes generated by the demolition of commercial properties is comprised mainly of brickwork and timber, in similar proportions as for housing wastes.

Table A.3 (a)

ESTIMATED COMPOSITION OF WASTES FROM CONSTRUCTION AND DEMOLITION WORKS — BELGIUM AND LUXEMBOURG

Year	DEMOLITION WASTE (% by weight)						Construction Waste	CONSTRUCTION AND DEMOLITION (% by weight)						
	Masonry	Concrete		Steel	Timber	Gypsum and Plaster		Masonry	Concrete		Steel	Timber	Gypsum and Plaster	Earth Works
		Plain	Reinforced						Plain	Reinforced				
1970	59	23	8	5	3	2	Mostly excavation material (earth, soil, stones, old tree-stumps, etc.)	28	11	4	2.4	1.4	1	52.2
1971	57	24	8.6	5.8	2.8	1.8		23	10	3.5	2.4	1.1	1	59
1972	59	23	8	5	3	2		24	9	3.2	2	1.2	1	59.6
1973	58	24	8	5	3	2		23	9.5	3	2	1.2	1	60.3
1974	55	25	10	6.5	2	1.5		21	9.6	4	2.5	.8	.6	61.5
1975	49	28	12	8	1.8	1.2		18	10	4.5	3	.7	.5	63.3

The composition of demolition and construction wastes in Denmark is thus as shown in Table A.3(b).

Table A.3(b)					
COMPOSITION OF DEMOLITION AND CONSTRUCTION WASTES - DENMARK					
	Demolition Wastes (i)			Construction Wastes	
Year	Materials arising (tonnes)	Brickwork	Timber	Materials arising	Constituent materials
		% by weight			
1978	108,000	90	10	N/A	mainly excavation material
(i) Excludes non-residential demolition waste other than from the demolition of commercial buildings.					

A.3.3   France

Of the contractors interviewed, three were able to apportion (by weight) the most significant materials arising from demolition works. These figures are given in Table A.3(c).

Table A.3(c)								
COMPOSITION OF DEMOLITION WASTE - FRANCE								
Contractor	Types of structures demolished as %		Proportion of materials arising % by weight					
	Housing and Commercial	Industrial	Brick	Stone	Concrete	Timber	Steel	Diverse
A	85	15	←——— 80* ———→			4	1	15
B	80	20	←——40→		40	*	1	*
C	90	10	25	44	20	4	1	5
* mostly masonry, little concrete								

The compositions of the waste are also changing rapidly with time. One contractor mentioned that concrete arisings accounted for about 15-20% of his total wastes until recently. The current proportion is nearer 40% and he believes that within a very few years this will increase to about 75%.

However, as a rough guide to the present situation, we estimate that about 60% of the current arisings from demolition are due to masonry (brick and stone), a maximum of 30% due to concrete, 1% to ferrous material and no more than 4% due to timber.   Most of the ferrous material will be reclaimed by the demolition contractor, and it is assumed that all of the other constituent materials are disposed of at tipping sites.

A.3.4   Federal Republic of Germany

Of the 72 million tonnes of demolition and construction waste that were generated in Germany in 1975, about 50% originated from demolition   (see Appendix A.2.4) and the remainder was comprised mainly of excavation wastes.

As to the material content of this waste, opinions differ as to the amount of concrete waste arising. The subjective opinions conveyed to us indicate a breakdown of demolition wastes as follows:

-        Concrete   - 9 million tonnes per annum
                            (of which around 70% is reinforced
                            concrete)

-        Timber   - 1 million tonnes per annum

-        Other (brick,
         stone, etc.)   - 26 million tonnes per annum

It was stated that 2.5 tonnes of reinforced concrete contains about 50kg of steel and the ferrous content in the waste, assuming no recovery of steel reinforcing, is thus approximately 125,000 tonnes each year.

Table A.3(d)

COMPOSITION OF DEMOLITION AND CONSTRUCTION WASTE IN THE FEDERAL REPUBLIC OF GERMANY - 1975

	Demolition Waste					Construction Waste	
Quantity (000 tonnes)	Proportion by material (% by weight)					Quantity (000 tonnes)	Excavation waste (earth, soil, rocks, etc.)
	Concrete		Timber	Ferrous	Other (mainly brick & stone)		
	Plain	Reinforced					
36,000	7.5	17.5	3	.35	72	36,000	virtually 100%

Table A.3(e)

PROPORTION BY WEIGHT OF MATERIALS GENERATED BY DEMOLITION IN ITALY

Date of Construction	Residential					Non-residential				
				Concrete					Concrete	
	Masonry	Timber	Iron and Steel	Plain	Reinforced	Masonry	Timber	Iron and Steel	Plain	Reinforced
pre 1885	80	20	–	–	–	80	20	–	–	–
1885–1905	89	10	1	–	–	90	8	2	–	–
1905–1925	85	8	2	5	–	80	5	4	10	–
post 1925	65	5	5	20	5	18	2	10	40	30

125

Our estimates for the composition of demolition and construction wastes are thus as shown in Table A.3(d).

A.3.5   Ireland

It is assumed that the composition of waste from residential demolition in Ireland is similar to that found in the United Kingdom, see Appendix A.3.8.

A.3.6   Italy

For both the residential and non-residential sectors, the composition is predominantly solid brick or stone, with wooden beams and floor joists. Between 1890 and 1910, some iron beams were used, followed by the increasing use of steel until 1925. After this date there was wide use of reinforced concrete and hollow, light-weight large size bricks with negligible structural timber work.

We cannot accurately detail the contribution that each material makes to the total material content of a building in each year class, but as the brief history given above is similar to that of other Community Member States, we have estimated the composition of buildings in each year class as shown in Table A.3(e), basing these figures on a wide range of discussions undertaken throughout the Community.

Using these figures, we have estimated demolition waste composition as shown in Table A.3(f). Wastes arising from new construction are mainly comprised of excavation material.

Table A.3(f)				
COMPOSITION OF WASTES ARISING FROM DEMOLITION AND CONSTRUCTION IN ITALY (% by weight)				
Material	From Residential demolition	From Non-Residential demolition	All Demolition	New Construction
Masonry	80	63	72	Mostly
Timber	13	8	10	earth and
Plain Concrete	4	15	10	soil,
Reinforced Concrete	1	10	5	stones, old
Iron and Steel	2	4	3	tree-stumps, etc.

Table A.3(g)

COMPOSITION OF DEMOLITION AND CONSTRUCTION WASTES IN THE NETHERLANDS - SAMPLE SURVEY 1976

Material	Volume %*	Assumed Density t/m^3	Weight Fraction %
Diverse hard material, most masonry	2	1.	37
Earth and stones	19	1.2	27
Wood	17	O.2	4
Concrete (plain and reinforced)	1O	1.3	15
Plastic products	2½	O.1	O.3
Asphalt**	1½	1.2	2
Metals	1½	O.2	O.3
Mixed housing waste (Fittings, etc.)***	1O	O.5	6
Mixed factory waste ****	14½	O.5	8.4

*   Source: SVA/1759 Bouw-en Sloopapval 1976.

**   Assumed due to road making and repair.

***   Includes fittings, floor coverings, wall-paper, tiles, glass, etc.

****   Includes old tree-stumps and branches, mud, agricultural wastes.

A.3.7 The Netherlands

In 1976, the SVA sampled loads of demolition* wastes arriving at tipping sites throughout the country. The results of this survey are reproduced in Table A.3(g). Also given in this table, are our assumptions of the density of each component of the wastes and the resulting composition by weight of the wastes.

The figures given above refer only to those materials taken for disposal to tipping sites. They do not include the large quantities of excavation material that are generated each year and which are mostly re-used on the construction site, at nearby sites, or for covering material, embankments, road making, etc.

A.3.8 United Kingdom

Appendix A.2.8 contains information on the composition of wastes arising form residential demolition. For the non-residential sector, we have used data obtained by the Building Research Establishment from a postal survey of demolition contractors (10). This data is included in Appendix A.3.1.

Our estimates for the composition of demolition wastes are thus as shown in Table A.3(h).

Table A.3(h)			
ESTIMATED COMPOSITION OF DEMOLITION WASTES IN THE UNITED KINGDOM (% by weight)			
Material	From residential demolition	From non-residential demolition	All Demolition
Masonry	70	29	40
Plain concrete	20	36	32
Reinforced concrete	Negligible	21	15
Timber	2.5	Negligible	1
Steel	Negligible	14*	10
Various (fittings,etc.)	7.5	N/A	2
* Almost all of this steel is structural steel that is reclaimed, rather than reinforcing steelwork, much of which is lost.			

---

* It is assumed that this relates to both demolition and construction wastes.

Appendix 4. Regional estimates of arisings of demolition and construction waste for each country

Table A.4(a)

ESTIMATED WASTE ARISINGS FROM CONSTRUCTION AND DEMOLITION — BELGIUM AND LUXEMBOURG 1975

	Construction Waste mainly earthworks '000 tonnes	Masonry	Plain Concrete	Reinforced Concrete (i)	Steel (ii)	Timber	Gypsum and Plaster	All materials '000 tonnes
Brussels	139	40	22	10	7	1.5	1.1	220.6
Walloon	424	120	67	30	20	5	3.4	669.4
Flemish	732	208	116	52	35	8	6	1,157
Belgium	1,295	368	205	92	62	14.5	10.5	2,047
Luxembourg	38	6.3	1.2	N/A	N/A	0.4	0.3	46

(i) Almost all steel in reinforced concrete is lost (approximately 20 kg. steel per tonne of reinforced concrete).

(ii) Close to 100% of this easily accessible steel is reclaimed.

Table A.4 (b)

ESTIMATED WASTE ARISINGS FROM DEMOLITION AND REHABILITATION – DENMARK 1978

Waste Arisings (Tonnes Per Annum)

Source	Copenhagen Area			Rest of Country			Denmark		
	Brickwork	Timber	Concrete Steel	Brickwork	Timber	Concrete Steel	Brickwork	Timber	Concrete Steel
Housing demolition	31,980	3,690	Negligible	20,020	2,310	Negligible	52,000	6,000	Negligible
Housing rehabilitation	1,454	727	Negligible	1,796	898	Negligible	3,250	1,625	Negligible
Commercial demolition *	16,000	2,000	Negligible	29,000	3,000	Negligible	45,000	5,000	Negligible
Industrial demolition	N/A	N/A	N/A N/A	N/A	N/A	N/A N/A	N/A	N/A	N/A N/A
TOTAL	49,434	6,417	N/A N/A	50,816	6,208	N/A N/A	100,250	12,625	N/A N/A

N/A = not available
* Based on regional population of Copenhagen (1.77 millions) compared to national population of 5.06 millions.
  Source: Eurostat 1977

Table A.4(c)

ESTIMATED WASTE ARISINGS FROM CONSTRUCTION AND DEMOLITION -
FRANCE 1977

Region	Construction Waste 1,000 tonnes	Demolition Waste * 1,000 tonnes				
	Earth, soil, stones, tree-stumps, etc.	Masonry	Plain and Reinforced Concrete	Timber	Diverse	Steel**
Ile de France	3,590	1,168	584	82	118	20
Parisian Basin	3,500	1,140	575	82	118	19
North-Pas-de-Calais	1,420	465	228	27	46	8
East	1,780	584	301	36	55	9
West	2,500	821	410	55	82	14
South West	2,020	657	328	46	64	11
Middle East	2,220	720	365	46	73	12
Mediter-ranean	2,007	675	337	46	64	11
France	19,100	6,230	3,128	420	620	104

* Includes repair, rehabilitiation and reconstruction wastes.

** Almost all ferrous material is reclaimed, other than the steel contained in reinforced concrete.

Table A.4(d)				
ESTIMATED WASTE ARISINGS FROM CONSTRUCTION AND DEMOLITION - FEDERAL REPUBLIC OF GERMANY - 1975				
Region	Demolition Wastes - '000 Tonnes*			Construction Waste '000 tonnes
	Concrete	Other	Total	
Schleswig-Holstein	480	950	1,430	1,430
Hamburg	320	640	960	960
Lower Saxony	340	2,680	4,020	4,020
Bremen	130	270	400	400
North Rhine-Westphalia	3,170	6,350	9,520	9,520
Hesse	1,030	2,050	3,080	3,080
Rhineland-Pflaz	680	1,360	2,040	2,040
Baden-Württemburg	1,700	3,390	5,090	5,090
Bavaria	2,000	4,000	6,000	6,000
Saarland	200	410	610	610
Berlin (West)**	950	1,900	2,850	2,850
Total (FRG)	12,000	24,000	36,000	36,000

* Includes repair, rehabilitation and reconstruction wastes

** 1977 figures

	Table A.4 (e)

ESTIMATED WASTE ARISINGS FROM CONSTRUCTION AND DEMOLITION –
IRELAND 1976

Region	Demolition Waste (tonnes)			Wastes (i) from Rehabilitation and Reconstruction (tonnes)	Construction Waste
	Concrete	Masonry	Total Demolition Waste		
Dublin	1,350	5,400	6,870	687	60,600
Rest of Country	6,666	26,664	33,930	3,393	299,400
Ireland	8,016	32,064	40,080	4,008	360,000

(i)   See text for assumptions

Table A.4(f)

ESTIMATED WASTE ARISINGS FROM CONSTRUCTION AND DEMOLITION – ITALY 1977

| Region | Demolition Wastes (1000 tonnes) | | | | | Per capita arisings of demolition waste kg/inhabitant | Rehabilitation and Reconstruction Wastes (1000 tonnes) | Construction Wastes 1000 (tonnes) |
	Masonry	Plain Concrete	Reinforced Concrete	Timber	Iron and Steel			
North-West	66	8	4	8	2	13	8	210
Lombardy	131	18	9	18	6	21	18	290
North East	149	20	10	20	6	32	20	210
Emilia – Romagna	94	13	7	13	4	33	13	130
Centre	23	3	2	3	1	6	3	190
Lazio	2	1	1	1	1	0.4	1	160
Campania	4	1	1	1	1	0.8	1	170
Abruzzi-Molise	5	1	1	1	1	3	1	50
Souk	28	4	2	4	1	6	4	210
Sicily	25	3	2	3	1	7	3	160
Sardinia	13	2	1	2	1	12	2	50
Italy	540	71	37	71	22	13	71	1830

Table A.4(g)

ESTIMATED WASTE ARISINGS FROM CONSTRUCTION AND DEMOLITION – NETHERLANDS 1976

Wastes Tipped – 1,000 Tonnes

Province	Masonry	Concrete	Wood	Asphalt	Metals	Soil, earth, etc.	Diverse	All Construction and Demolition
Groningen	57	23	6	3	0.5	41	22	153
Friesland	45	18	5	3	0.4	33	18	121
Drenthe	38	15	4	2	0.3	28	15	102
Overjissel	56	23	6	3	0.5	40	22	151
Gelderland	217	88	23	12	1.8	158	86	586
Utrecht	164	67	18	9	1.3	120	65	444
N. Holland	447	181	48	24	3.6	326	177	1,207
S. Holland	653	265	71	35	5.3	476	259	1,764
Zeeland	124	50	13	7	1.0	90	49	334
N. Brabant	365	148	39	20	3.0	266	145	986
Limburg	462	187	50	25	3.7	337	184	1,249
Netherlands	2,628	1,065	283	143	21.4	1,915	1,042	7,097

Table A.4(h)(i)			
RESIDENTIAL DEMOLITIONS BY REGIONS — U.K.			
Region	Average annual dwellings demolished 1968 - 1976	Population '000s	Dwellings demolished per 1,000 inhabitants
England & Wales	63,000	49,299	1.3
Scotland	15,000	5,206	2.9
Northern Ireland	5,000	1,537	3.3
U.K.	83,000	56,042	1.5

Table A.4(h)(ii)							
ESTIMATED WASTE ARISINGS FROM CONSTRUCTION AND DEMOLITION — UNITED KINGDOM 1978							
Region	Demolition Waste (1,000 Tonnes)						Construction Waste (1,000t) (mostly earth, soil, stones, etc.)
	Masonry	Plain Concrete	Reinforced Concrete	Timber	Steel	All Materials	
G.L.C.	902	693	330	15	220	2,200	2,500
England excl. G.L.C.	5,084	3,906	1,860	87	1,240	12,400	14,300
Wales	369	284	135	6	90	900	1,000
Scotland	1,353	1,039	495	23	330	3,300	3,800
Northern Ireland	492	378	180	8	120	1,200	1,400
U.K.	8,200	6,300	3,000	140	2,000	20,000	23,000

136

Appendix 5. Costs of transporting demolition wastes in different EEC countries, as reported by contractors

Table A.5 (a)

COSTS OF TRANSPORTING DEMOLITION WASTES IN DIFFERENT EEC COUNTRIES,
AS REPORTED BY CONTRACTORS

Country	Nature of Material	Cost figure quoted	Cost per tonne /kilometre, one-way (i)	Comments
Belgium	Mixed rubble	BF750-1,000 per hour for truck	BF4-5	
France	Mixed rubble	FF0.35 per tonne/kilo-meter	FF0.35	In Paris area up to 50 kms. distance to tip
France	Mixed rubble	FF500-600 per day per truck	FF0.33-0.40	Own truck in Paris area
France	Mixed rubble	FF950 per day per truck	FF0.63	Hired truck in Paris area
France	Mixed rubble	FF800 per day per truck	FF0.53	Own truck in Paris area
Denmark	Mixed rubble	DKr200 per day per 15t truck	DKr1.07	
Italy	Mixed rubble	L200 per tonne /kilometre	L200	
Germany	Mixed rubble	DM6-8/m^3 for 15-20 kms. distance	DM0.25-0.44	
Germany	Mixed rubble	DM11.20/m^3 for 15 kms. distance	DM0.62	In Duisberg area
Germany	Unbroken concrete	DM36/t for 50kms. distance	DM0.72	
U.K.	Mixed rubble	£10.00 per hour per 20t truck	£0.04	In London area
U.K.	Mixed rubble	£5.50 per hour per 10t truck	£0.04	

Table A.5.(a) - Sheet 2

COSTS OF TRANSPORTING DEMOLITION WASTES IN DIFFERENT EEC COUNTRIES,
AS REPORTED BY CONTRACTORS

Country	Nature of Material	Cost figure quoted	Cost per tonne /kilometre, one-way (i)	Comments
Netherlands	Mixed rubble	fl.12.5/tonne for 25kms. distance	fl.0.50	10t. truck
Netherlands	Mixed rubble	fl.10/tonne for 25kms. distance	fl.0.40	20t. truck
Netherlands	Mixed Rubble	fl.5-10/tonne for 15kms. distance	fl.0.33-0.66	

Range of costs indicated $0.08 - $0.39 per tonne/kilometre

Note (i) Unless otherwise indicated by the figure quoted, we have
calculated costs per tonne/kilometre on the basis of an
8 hour round-trip and a distance to tip of 25 kms.

Appendix 6. Operating costs for an 8 tonne and 20 tonne capacity truck in the Netherlands

Table A.6(a)		
OPERATING COSTS FOR AN 8 TONNE AND 20 TONNE CAPACITY TRUCK IN THE NETHERLANDS		
	8 tonne truck	20 tonne truck
STANDING COSTS	$ per week	$ per week
Wages/Employee expenses	560	620
Insurance	30	42
Taxes	30	50
Garage charges	10	10
Overhead	175	350
Depreciation	65	150
Interest charges	55	76
TOTAL	925	1,298
RUNNING COSTS	$ per kilometre	$ per kilometre
Fuel	.08	.09
Lubricants/tyres	.04	.04
Repairs/maintenance	.10	.12
TOTAL	.22	.25
Sources: Koninklijke Nederlandse Vereniging van Transport-Ondernemingen KNVTO. Aannemingsbedrijf Van Eck C.V., Den Haag.		

Appendix 7. (i) **Operating features of some existing demolition waste processing/recovery plants;**

(ii) **Comparison of calculated and actual production costs of aggregate recovery from concrete waste – U.S.A.**

Table A.7.(a)

OPERATING FEATURES OF SOME EXISTING DEMOLITION WASTE PROCESSING/RECOVERY PLANTS

Plant	Types of Waste Accepted	Size of Plant Site in m²	Average Production Rate in tph	Types of Equipment used	Number of Personnel	Products of plant
Hamburg (Rothernburgsort) FRG	Mixed rubble. Brick preferred. Small quantities of plain concrete	8,000	100	- impact crusher - jaw crusher - screen - washer - bulldozer - storage silos	4 - 5	- rubble sand (u3) - fine crushed brick (<10mm) - brick grit (3/15mm & 15/30mm) - broken brick ballast (30/60mm & 60/200mm) - Wall debris for con- struction roads.
West Drayton, U.K.	Concrete pavement, mixed brick and con- crete brick. (not wood or other contaminated rubble). Can handle limited reinforced concrete	16,000	90-100	- jaw crusher - 2 shovel loaders - hydraulic impact hammer	5	- fine aggregate - coarse aggregate

Table A.7.(a) - Sheet 2

OPERATING FEATURES OF SOME EXISTING DEMOLITION WASTE PROCESSING/RECOVERY PLANTS

Plant	Types of Waste Accepted	Size of Plant Site in m²	Average Production Rate in tph	Types of Equipment used	Number of Personnel	Products of plant
Scratchwood, U.K.	Will accept virtually anything. (Wood burnt on-site to crack concrete masses).	ca 8,000	50-60	- small jaw crusher - 2 shovel loaders	4	- fine aggregate (contaminated) - coarse aggregate (contaminated)
G.F. Atkinson & Co. Long Beach Interchange Project, California, U.S.A.	Concrete pavement	na	150	- primary jaw crusher - secondary cone crusher - screen	na	- <20mm aggregate
City of Minneapolis Recycling Plant, USA.	Plain concrete, mixed brick and concrete	na	200	- primary jaw crusher - secondary cone crusher - screen	na	- <25 aggregate
Reclaimed Aggregate Co., Washington D.C., U.S.A.	Plain concrete, mixed brick and concrete	na	100-200	- jaw crusher - screen	na	- 50mm aggregate

Table A.7.(b)			
COMPARISON OF CALCULATED AND ACTUAL PRODUCTION COSTS OF AGGREGATE RECOVERY FROM CONCRETE WASTE - U.S.A.			
Project	Average Production Rate in Tonnes Per Hour	Calculated Production Cost in $ Per Tonne - 1976*	Actual Production Cost in $ Per Tonne
Long Beach Interchange Project, California**	150	1.64	1.45 (1971)
118/5 Interchange Project California**	250	1.30	1.32 (1976)
City of Minneapolis Recycling Plant	200	1.42	1.20 (1972)
Redondo Beach Freeway Project, California ***			

Notes: *   Assuming 1,429 hours of plant operation per year.

        **   G.F. Atkinson Company.

      ***   Kasler Corporation.

Appendix 8. Public authorities and research organisations concerned with demolition, use of materials and disposal

A.8.1   Public Authorities

In most of the Member States of the Community, there is an under-
standable reluctance for central authorities to be particularly
concerned with problems of recovery or disposal of demolition
waste materials - there are many other secondary materials and
waste disposal problems which must take higher priority. However,
national authorities are aware that problems are likely to
arise in the future when demolition of the newer generation of
large reinforced and pre-stressed buildings becomes common.

We cite below the various national, regional and local authorities
in each country that have competence in the fields of demolition,
use of materials and disposal.

A.8.1.1   Belgium

Two Ministries in particular are responsible for the deposition
and treatment of solid wastes, the Ministry of Public Health
and the Environment and the Ministry of Labour.

The Ministry of Labour has competence for most industrial wastes
but some such wastes, including those from demolition and
construction fall under the competence of the Ministry of Public
Health. Powers pertaining to the deposition and treatment of
these latter wastes have now passed to regional authorities.

A.8.1.2   France

The "Ministère de l'Environnement et de l'Equipement" may be
consulted when explosives are to be used for demolition, and
the "Ministère des Affaires Culturelles" is consulted when listed
houses or conservation areas are being considered. In such
cases special permits from the relevant Ministries are required.

The "Ministère de Travail" imposes regulations under a decree of
8th January, 1965, relating to health and safety measures. These
regulations are strictly enforced by an Inspectorate - "Les
inspecteurs de travail" - and fines can be quite large and
imposed firmly. Prison sentences may also be given, although
this is more unlikely.

Environmental constraints are not imposed upon the industry by
central government, although demolition companies are supposed
to work with "social conscience and a sense of responsibility".

Other than in these areas, central government does not normally become involved with demolition problems. As far as the waste materials are concerned, central government does not see demolition and construction wastes as a priority problem. It was pointed out to us that there is a sufficiency of available tipping space in France for inert wastes such as these, and although demolition companies may have to transport wastes further afield in the future, no shortage of land for tipping is foreseen.

Control over disposal on land is exercised only in those communes for which there is a town and country development plan, and competence for disposal of these wastes is vested with the communal authorities (normally the mayor).

Competence for disposal of demolition and construction wastes is vested with regional authorities. However, landfill sites are often privately owned and run, especially those which accept industrial wastes. A tipping permit (permit de versage) is required from the regional authority in order to open, or extend, a private disposal site. Once this has been granted and providing there are few complaints from residents, the authority often has no further interest in the operation of the site.

A.8.1.3   Denmark

Both the Ministries of the Environment and of Housing have an effect on demolition practice and disposal. The Ministry of the Environment is mainly concerned with the disposal of the wastes, but also affects demolition practice in that it establishes policy on all matters that may affect the environment, even temporarily. Furthermore, the Minister can now affect materials usage under the Law on Raw Materials (1977).

The Ministry of Housing has a great effect on the numbers of dwellings demolished via policy decision and laws such as the Slum Clearance Law. Similarly, the Building Law (1975) affects the quality of materials used in construction, and thus the potential for recovery of secondary materials.

Possibly the major organisations concerned with demolition are the Slum Clearance Agencies. There are two such companies, one which formulates rehabilitation or demolition plans for publicly-owned dwellings, and another which is concerned with privately-owned buildings. These organisations are both State funded. They are responsible for the planning, negotiation and administration of most of the slum clearance and town renewal work in Denmark.

Local authorities are responsible for the disposal of wastes on land. They may also lay down rules on the operation of tips including directives on pre-treatment by size-reduction methods.

A.8.1.4   Federal Republic of Germany

At the Federal level, several ministries have competence concerning different aspects of demolition, use of materials, transport and disposal of wastes. There are, in addition, a

146

number of separate Federal agencies which operate under the jurisdiction of a Federal Minister.

The Bundesministerium des Innern (Federal Ministry of the Interior) is the ministry primarily responsible for the development and supervision of national policy and legislation in respect of environmental protection and waste management. The Umweltbundesamt (Federal Environment Agency) is an agency of the Ministry of the Interior with the role of providing expert advice on matters concerning the environment, including waste management, and implementing and co-ordinating research in this area. Similarly, the Statistisches Bundesamt (Federal Statistical Office) is concerned with the compilation of information and national statistics on waste production and disposal.

The Bundesministerium für Wirtschaft (Federal Ministry for Economic Affairs) and its related agencies the Bundesamt für Gewerbliche Wirtschaft (Federal Agency for Commercial Affairs), the Bundesanstalt für Geowissenschaften und Rohstoffe (Federal Agency for Geological Sciences and Raw Materials), and the Bundesanstalt für Materialprüfung (Federal Agency for Materials Testing), maintain an interest in matters related to the supply of raw materials and the recovery and use of secondary raw materials.

The Bundesministerium für Verkehr (Federal Ministry for Transport) is responsible for developing national policy and legislation relating to transport and for constituting a number of Commissions to administer regulations on tariffs for short-haul road transport. Of particular interest for demolition waste transport is the Tarifkommission des allgemeinen Güternahverkehrs (TKN), which oversees the Tarif für den Güternahverkehr mit Kraftfahrzeugen (Tariff for Short-Haul Transport of Goods in Motor Vehicles). The Bundesanstalt für Strassenwesen (Federal Agency for Road Construction) is principally active in the field of road research, including the use of materials recovered from waste in road construction.

The Bundesministerium für Forschung und Technologie (Federal Ministry of Research and Technology) promotes and supports research in the field of waste management.

The Laender (states) have an important role in that they provide detailed implementing legislation at the state level in furtherance of framework Federal legislation. They are also responsible for preparing long-term waste management plans for their areas.

The Regierungsbezirke (regional government authorities), being subsidiary authorities of the Laender, are involved in overseeing the implementation of the state waste management plan, and in administering the approvals and licences for the transport and disposal of wastes.

Most disposal sites are owned and operated by the local authorities, though some are operated by private firms on behalf of local authorities. There are, nevertheless, quite a number of privately owned and operated disposal sites, which require licensing by the regional government authority.

A.8.1.5   Ireland

Several central government agencies in Ireland have competence covering different aspects of demolition, use of materials, transport and disposal of wastes. The Department of the Environment and Ministry of Local Government are primarily responsible for the development and supervision of national policy concerning the prohibition, regulation and control of the deposit and disposal of waste materials. The Ministry of Industry and Commerce through the Industrial Development Authority (IDA), has a policy of dispersing grants to Irish and foreign manufacturers and recently established a Project Identification Section whose function is to recognise opportunities to substitute imports with home produced goods. There is currently much interest in this Section in resource recovery from wastes.

Disposal of wastes on land is the responsibility of local authorities. Apart from areas immediately surrounding the larger cities, most disposal of construction and demolition wastes is uncontrolled.

A.8.1.6   Italy

There is no particular interest at national level in problems associated with demolition and construction wastes. The regional governments do have special powers over environmental problems, but they are not yet sufficiently geared-up (in terms of qualified staff and expertise) to have examined the environmental effects associated with these wastes. The Regional Government of Lombardy did, however, state that it did not consider waste arisings from construction and demolition to be a serious problem at the present time.

It is at the "commune" or local authority level that most control over demolition and construction practice exists. A demolition licence is required from the Planning Authorities of the commune. This licence is a form issued by the Italian Statistical Institute and it is because of this that statistics on demolition in Italy are exceptionally coherent and accurate.

The Public Works Committee of the commune is responsible for the decision to allow demolition. In the particular case of residential demolition, the opinions of the Town Planning Committee and the Fine Arts Committee of the Regional Government must be sought.

As far as waste disposal is concerned, most industrial waste is taken to private owned tips. Very few communes have facilities for industrial wastes. Construction waste and demolition rubble is normally sought after for use as foundation and covering material and in general the only components of these wastes that are tipped are insect and nail-infested wood, plastics and reinforced concrete.

A.8.1.7   Luxembourg

At the present time, neither central nor local authorities in the Grand Duchy have much interest in demolition and construction wastes. The quantity of such wastes arising in Luxembourg is small and no problems have been encountered with their disposal.

The Ministry of Public Health and the Environment is responsible for policy concerning the environment and for the instigation and funding of particular research programmes. We have no knowledge of any such work being undertaken in the field of demolition and construction wastes.

The Ministry of the Interior is responsible for the authorisation of waste depots, but there are in general no provisions governing the place where industrial wastes are to be discharged.

Communal authorities are the relevant authorities concerned with solid waste disposal. In 1971, the intercommunal syndicate for waste disposal of the cantons of Luxembourg, Esch and Capellen was formed with the intention of reducing the amount of uncontrolled discharge. In 1974, the Luxembourg authorities expressed the intention of prohibiting uncontrolled waste disposal in the future and taking severe action to prevent the dumping of rubbish in the open countryside. It is unclear what effect such policy is having upon demolition and construction wastes but it appears that these wastes still today are mostly disposed of by uncontrolled tipping.

A.8.1.8   The Netherlands

Dutch authorities, both central and regional, are much more interested in the problems associated with waste materials from construction and demolition than are authorities of other Member States. The principal reason for this is the acute shortage of available disposal sites in the densely populated western part of the country, allied to national regulations forbidding the transport of industrial wastes generated in one province to disposal areas situated in another province.

The National Government, acting through an Inter-Ministerial Committee on Wastes, formulates policy proposals. This committee is made up of the Ministries of Economic Affairs, Environment and Public Health, Transport and Road Building, and Housing and Planning. It receives advice from various research organisations, and direct funds from the individual ministries towards particular research topics. It is the responsibility of the individual ministry concerned to act on the policies proposed and to formulate legislation. The provincial governments are then required to implement this legislation.

A.8.1.9   The United Kingdom

There is little Central Government interest in demolition practice. The main forms of control are DDIR, the Codes of Practice, and the Health and Safety at Work Regulations. Permission for demolition is usually viewed as a planning matter (e.g. application for change of use of the building), and local building regulations and standards for use of materials apply. These functions are administered by local authorities who are better aware of the local conditions and social acceptability of the project.

The Department of the Environment is currently investigating questions associated with the demand, resources and extraction of natural aggregates, but it does not feel that demolition hardcore will ever become a significant substitute product, except possibly on a very localised basis. The DoE gives as reasons for such beliefs the problems associated with storage, the cost of processing and transport, and the problem of spasmodic occurrence.

Disposal of demolition wastes by local authorities is undertaken very much on an ad hoc basis. Almost all public tips will accept demolition and construction waste. Tipping charges will vary dependent upon tip availability and requirement for covering material. Very often high concentrations of timber are discouraged (e.g. by higher charges).

A.8.2   Research organisations

The amount of research work being undertaken in the Community on problems associated with demolition and the use of materials is small. We cite below organisations that have either undertaken work in this field, or that have expressed interest in these fields.

A.8.2.1   Belgium

The major research organisation concerned with problems arising from demolition and demolition waste materials in Belgium is the Centre Scientifique et Technique de la Construction (CSTC). This organisation is financed mainly from the construction industry, but also receives some government funding. At the present time it is involved in projects concerned with the demolition and re-use of concrete, together with organisations from two other countries, the Netherlands and Germany. Funding for the Belgian part of this work is being supplied by both the CSTC and the Ministry of Economic Affairs.

The Belgian Road Research Institute - the "Centre de Récherches Routières" is also interested in the re-use of wastes from the demolition or repair of roads. It co-operated with an OECD research group which studied the use of waste materials and by-products in road construction.

A.8.2.2   Denmark

Various research organisations advise central authorities on problems concerned with demolition, and the recovery of demolition and construction materials. These include the Building Research Institute, the Technological Institute and experts from such universities as the Technical High School.

A.8.2.3   France

The major research organisation concerned with the reclamation, recycling and re-use of demolition and construction wastes is the "Réunion Internationale des Laboratoires d'Essais et de Récherches sur les Matériaux et les Construction (R.I.L.E.M.). This organisation brings together international experts on various subjects dealing with materials and construction in the form of R.I.L.E.M. committees, which investigate and report on particular topics. There is currently a R.I.L.E.M. committee concerned with the demolition and re-use of concrete.

Other research organisations concerned with construction materials and wastes are the "Centre Scientifique et Technique du Bâtiment" (C.S.T.B.), the "Laboratoires des Ponts et Chaussées", the "Centre Experimental de Récherches et d'Etudes du Bâtiment et des Travaux Publiques" (C.E.B.T.P.) and the "Centre Technique du Bois" (C.T.B.).

A.8.2.4   Federal Republic of Germany

At the national level, the Deutscher Ausschuss für Stahlbeton (German Committee for Reinforced Concrete), an affiliated body of the German Standards Institute (DIN), has been investigating new techniques for dismantling concrete structures and for recycling and disposing of the waste materials. The Forschungs Institut der Zementindustrie (the Research Institute of the Cement Industry) also maintains an interest in the demolition and recycling of concrete.

A.8.2.5   Ireland

Two main organisations act as advisory bodies to central authorities - the National Institute for Physical Planning and Construction Research, and the Institute for Industrial Research and Standards (IRRS). The IRRS, apart from instigating and administering research effort, is also responsible for the establishment of standards for building materials.

A.8.2.6   Italy

One particular organisation that is becoming interested in demolition problems is the Italian Building Materials Research Committee (CRESME). This organisation is financed by industry, and although to date it has not undertaken work concerned with demolition and construction wastes, we were informed that it is now proposed to monitor the sources, types and quantities of these materials.

A.8.2.7   The Netherlands

Central authorities are currently sponsoring several studies concerned with demolition wastes. These include involvement with organisations in Belgium and in Germany in projects concerned with the demolition and re-use of concrete. Other work being undertaken includes an examination of separation techniques, and quantitative assessments of national waste arisings. Much of this work is being undertaken by the Stichting Verwijdering Afvalstoffen (SVA). This organisation is wholly funded by National Government, and undertakes or manages projects concerned with all kinds of wastes.

A second public research organisation interested in these wastes is the Central Organisation for Applied Scientific Research (TNO). This organisation was provided for in an Act of Parliament in

1930, and established in 1932. It is funded by direct subsidy from the State and also by undertaking contractual work for both the public and private sectors. The Department of Building Materials is currently examining the possibility of using processed concrete wastes from demolition as a substitute for natural aggregates.

The Dutch Road Research Laboratory (Rijksvegenbouwlaboratorium) is also particularly interested in the reclamation and re-use of demolition wastes. Experts from this laboratory have already experimented with recycling asphalt wastes generated during road repair and are also examining the possibilities and problems of using crushed brick and concrete wastes in new road construction.

Private organisations that are interested in these subjects include cement and ready-mix concrete producers and the Building Centre (Bouwcentrum), which has undertaken a qualitative study of demolition waste arisings in conjunction with the Economic Institute for Building Activities (E.I.B.). Also, the Dutch Committee for Concrete Research (CUR) is currently involved in several projects concerned with demolition wastes. This organisation, in conjunction with the "Stichting Commissie voor Schriften Beton" (Standards Institute for Concrete) expects to undertake work in the near future on proposals on standards concerning the use of brick and concrete wastes from demolition in new concrete manufacture.

The Technological University of Eindhoven is investigating methods for reducing the energy requirement for fragmentation of concrete. At the Stevin Laboratory of the Technological University of Delft, work is underway to examine the extent to which demountable construction methods offer a meaningful alternative to present methods of construction.

A.8.2.8   United Kingdom

Research into new end-uses for demolition and construction waste materials is centred mainly in one organisation - the Building Research Establishment (BRE). It should be emphasised that even this organisation views the subject of construction and demolition wastes as a low priority subject. There has been some work undertaken at the BRE into new demolition methods and the BRE has, in fact, developed a novel machine for breaking concrete. This machine has recently been put on the market under licence.

Other workers at the BRE have studied the possibility of increasing the reclamation of certain constituents of demolition and construction wastes, for example the manufacture of new concrete from crushed concrete aggregate.

One further organisation which is interested in the recycling of demolition wastes is the Transport and Road Research Laboratory (TRRL). Workers at this laboratory have studied the use of various waste materials in road construction, including mixed rubble from demolition. They found demolition rubble to be a satisfactory substitute for natural aggregate for use as a sub-base material, but emphasised that this rubble must contain little or no contamination (as gypsum, timber, metals, etc.)

Appendix 9.   Review of relevant government regulations in the member states

A.9.1   <u>Belgium</u>

There is very little legislation in Belgium concerning the treatment and disposal of wastes from demolition and construction. The major texts that affect these wastes are the Regulations for the Protection of Labour (RGPT),and the Law relating to the development of the territory and town planning.

The RGPT (Decrees of the Regent of 11 February 1946 and 27 September 1947, modified by A.R. of 11 September 1970) provides that the erection, conversion or removal of various establishments must be authorised by the administration authorities. These establishments are enumerated in the Law in a list which actually comprises most industrial activities likely to cause pollution. The competent authority is dictated by the type of industrial activity.

The Law of 29 March 1962 (ammended by the Laws of 22 April 1970 and 22 December 1976) concerning the development of the territory provides that no person, without written permission from the College of the Burgomaster and Alderman,may appreciably alter the relief of the land.

Competence for treatment and deposition of solid wastes (including demolition and construction wastes) has recently been transferred to regional authorities under the Egmont Pact (Annex 1 of the Government Declaration of 7 June 1977, pp 33-34. In the authorisation for establishing tips, specific provisions may be laid down covering the restoration of the land.

More particular legislation includes provisions in the Law establishing Zones of Special Protection, (A.R. of 26 July 1971, modified by A.R. 3 July 1972) in which the burning of any wastes in open air is forbidden, except for wastes arising from gardening, agricultural or forestry work.

The dumping of any wastes is forbidden in natural reservations, Law of 12 July 1973, relating to the Conservation of Nature.

Regulation of toxic wastes in Belgium dates from the Arrêté Royal of 16 October 1972, when a heading of "toxic wastes" was introduced into list A of classified establishments of the RGPT. Although wastes from demolition and construction are not normally considered as toxic, demolition wastes impregnated with toxic industrial compounds (e.g. pesticides) could arise from a factory or warehouse fire, or other accident. Under the Law of 22 July 1974, the transport and disposal of toxic wastes is regulated, and the producer of the wastes is made responsible for all risks.

A.9.2   Denmark

Article 63 of the Nature Conservation Act (Statute No. 445 of 1 October 1972) forbids disposal of waste on other people's land without the permission of the owner.

In general, there are no other detailed provisions concerning the transport, treatment or disposal of inert solid wastes such as those that arise from construction and demolition work. The county or district councils are responsible for the siting of tips and waste treatment plant (Chapter 5, Environment Protection Regulation, No. 170 of 29 March 1974). A guide has been issued to the councils concerning approval of tips (Guidance No. 1/1974, Director of the Environment). If the storage, transport or disposal of such wastes becomes a serious nuisance, the district council can issue concrete orders as to special methods of storage and disposal.

More particular regulations which affect demolition and construction work include:

-    the Slum Clearance Law (originally No. 318 of 18/6/69. Updated several times in 1971, '73 and '75. Latest update is No. 356 of 3/7/75. The objectives of this law are to:

   i.   demolish or improve sub-standard and unhealthy dwellings;

   ii.   renovate old inner-city areas;

   iii. rehouse people who have lost homes due to this Act;

   iv.   give the necessary administrative and economic foundation for increased renewal activity.

-    the Law on the Protection of the Environment (No. 372 of 13/6/73) which sets a maximimum standard for noise pollution of 50 dB measured within a dwelling. However, condemnation or improvement cannot be forced using this law, the Town Renewal Law will be the operative one.

-    the Law of Housing Standards (No. 362 of 3/7/74) which gives rules for the minimum standards required of housing. Sub-standard dwellings may be condemned. The time allowed for improvement or demolition can vary between ½ and 12 years. However, no financial aid is available to the owner under this law for improvement or demolition.

- the Fire-Security Law (initially No. 53 but updated many times. The current regulations are combined in a Memorandum of 9/7/77.). This law specifies that any building of over two storeys which contains at least one dwelling unit must be fire-secured.

- the Building Law (No. 323 of 26/6/75) which affects the re-use of materials, as it pertains to the construction of new buildings. Regulations on Building Standards were introduced under this law in 1977 which specify material strengths required in new buildings.

- the Law on Raw Materials (No. 237 of 8/6/77). This law may have an affect on the future re-use of demolition waste materials as under Article 6, the Minister of the Environment, after discussions with the Ministers of Housing and Public Works can, in order to conserve resources or to assure an economic use of raw materials, make regulations about the quantity and quality of raw materials used in construction, or specify that replacement, recycled, or waste products be used in certain types of building and construction.

- the Town Renewal Plan. At present this is not a law. It is currently being discussed in Parliament. It will fall under and enhance the work of the Slum Clearance Act.

A.9.3.   France

Most of the regulations pertaining to control over deposits are set out in Decree No. 62-461 of 13/4/62, which deals with the various ways in which land may be used. Two orders, dated 25/4/63 , have been added to this decree. Land may only be allocated for the deposit of wastes if the relevant authority gives its prior consent. The user submits a request to the mayor of a commune, who formulates an opinion which is then passed on to the departmental services of plant and housing.

The siting, and operation of sites for the deposit or treatment of industrial wastes is regulated by the Law of 19 December 1917, relating to dangerous, unhealthy, or unfit establishments. These include establishments which produce waste, and those receiving wastes for disposal of treatment.

An order of 9/3/73 relating to the controlled discharge of urban wastes specifies that if the disposal site is equipped with crushing plant, it should be situated such that local residents are not affected by noise, vibration or dust.

A Decree of 8/1/65 relates to particular measures applicable for the protection of health in construction work. A special section relates to demolition work (Title 6, Articles 97-105). These regulations aim to improve the safety of construction and demolition work. Inspections are carried out by an inspectorate - "les inspectors de travail".

155

The main item of legislation which seeks principally to reduce
the amount of waste is the Law of 15/7/75 concerning the
Elimination of Wastes and Recovery of Materials (Law No. 75-633).
Under title V of the law, the elimination of wastes must be
carried out in conditions which facilitate the recovery of
materials or energy. The government can fix the minimum proportions of recovered materials or components which must be used in
the manufacture of a product or product category. In this context,
it is implicitly prohibited to descriminate against the presence
of recovered materials in products which satisfy regulations and
standards. The government may also regulate methods of using
materials, components or energy in order to facilitate subsequent
recovery.

A.9.4   Federal Republic of Germany

The most important legislative programme relating to solid waste
management in the Federal Republic is the 1972 Waste Law
(Abfallbeseitigungsgesetz). Under this law, the states are
required to prepare waste disposal plans, which are to contain
estimates of current and future waste arisings, responsibilites
for their disposal, and indications of where and when new
facilities may be required.

The state governments are allowed to enact state laws defining
which public authorities are to be responsible in the first
instance for the disposal of wastes (section 3, Abfg). In most
cases, the state governments have elected to make the Kreise
(local authorities) the "responsible public authorities". The
Abfg (section 3) further allows the "responsible authorities",
with the agreement of the state government, to exclude from their
disposal responsibilities "such wastes which, because of their
type or quantity, cannot be disposed of along with household
wastes". Where such wastes are excluded, the owner of these
wastes remains responsible for their proper disposal. The type,
quantity and composition of these latter wastes must be recorded
by the owner, and this information transmitted to an authority
designated by the state government (frequently the Regierungs
Präsidenten). The place of final disposal must also be given.

It is thus that "wild-cat" tipping of construction and demolition
wastes, and other forms of uncontrolled disposal, is virtually
eliminated in the Federal Republic.

A.9.5   Ireland

Responsibility for the control of deposits of wastes on land lies
almost entirely with local authorities in their various capacities.
The law governing such matters is highly fragmented and is contained
in a large number of statutes dating from the late nineteenth
century.

General control is covered by the Local Government (Planning and
Development) Act 1963. which empowers planning authorities to
include in development plans provisions for the prohibition,
regulation and control of the deposit and disposal of wastes.

Also, under this Act, it is an offence for any person to deposit any rubble or other rubbish so as to create or tend to create litter.

The Municipal Corporations (Ireland) Act, 1840 and the Local Government 'Ireland) 1898 Act empower local authorities to make bye-laws for the "good-rule and government" of their areas, and for the prevention and suppression of nuisances. Sanitary authorities may also make bye-laws relating to nuisances under the Public Health (Ireland) Act 1878.

Control of a more particular nature is effected by several statutes which include:

- the Rivers Pollution Prevention Acts 1876 and 1893. These prohibit the discharge of solid waste from any manufactory, manufacturing process or quarry into any "stream" so as to interfere with its flow or pollute its waters. A "stream" is defined as any river, stream, canal, lake or watercourse and may include such areas of the sea and tidal waters as the Minister for Local Government may define by order.

- the Harbours Act 1946. This Act makes it an offence for any person to dispose of ballast, earth, ashes, stones or any other substance within the limits of a harbour without the authorisation of the harbour authority.

- the Foreshore Act, 1933. This prohibits the dumping of waste on the foreshore.

Controls over housing demolition exist under the Local Government (Sanitary Services) Act 1964, which empowers local authorities to declare a building or structure unsafe. The Housing Acts 1966 and 1969, affect houses considered unfit for human habitation, and give the local authority powers of inspection. Orders for closure, demolition or repair may be made. There is no Legislation affecting the demolition of industrial premises.

A.9.6   Italy

Law No. 366 of 20/3/1941 is the only specific law governing the collection, transportation and disposal of solid wastes. The main purpose of this law was the re-employment in agriculture and in industry of waste substances and materials by means of suitable grading to eliminate loss.

In 1971, the Ecological Commission of the Senate presented a report on pollution by solid refuse in which it was stressed that the 1941 law had almost completely fallen into disuse.*

---

* Senate of the Republic – Special Commission on Ecological Problems. Report on pollution from solid wastes, the safe-guarding of marshland and pollution by noise. Doc.XXV, No.1 13.12.1971, p.21.

The central organs provided for in this law (a central office for collection, transport and disposal studies, research and promotional campaigns, and a central commission with advisory functions) were never set up, and the obligation of prior grading of refuse with a view to its re-use was never complied with.

Disposal of wastes from construction and demolition activity are regulated by Law No. 366. There is a general ban on discharging urban waste, and also on depositing it temporarily in public places, and on public or private ground. Plant for disposing of waste and for grading and recycling must be located at least one kilometer from the inhabited area.

Powers of supervision and control are enjoyed by the Minister of Health. However, administrative functions have not been transferred to the regions by a decree of 1972 (DPR 14.1.1972 No.4). Numerous regional laws have been issued allowing communes funds for the construction, extension or enlargement of services, incineration and transformation plant and controlled discharging locations. Examples of these are L.R. 19 November 1973 No. 23 of Campania, which takes over complete liability for the expenditure contemplated and LP 1973 No. 59 of Trento, in which priority campaigns are laid down in regard to the removal of polluting wastes, and the elimination of discharged materials from rivers and woods.

A.9.7   Luxembourg

There is no overall law covering the discharge of wastes on land in the Grand Duchy. Specific regulations are applicable to certain wastes, or to particular areas.

The Grand-ducal Decree of 17 June 1872 (amended by Decree of 7 July 1882) relates to establishments held to be dangerous, unhealthy, noxious or noisy. Authorities, when granting authorisation for the operation of such establishments, may add such reservations and conditions as are deemed necessary in the interests of public safety, health and convenience.

The Law of 29 July 1965 on the conservation of nature and of natural resources forbids the abandonment, dumping or discharge of any kind of waste on the public highway, or on land belonging to a third party, other than at a site specifically designated for this purpose by the communal authorities.

The Law of 27 June 1906 on the protection of public health lays the obligation on the communes to make provision for the disposal of waste matter.

Possibilities for research programmes concerning the deposition, or the potential for reclamation of construction and demolition wastes exist under the governmental declaration of 4 July 1974, in which the Ministry of Public Health and the Environment is to realise progressively a programme of study and work in the field of environmental protection.

A.9.8   The Netherlands

The Nuisance Act (1952 Stb 274) prohibits the establishment,
operation, extension or alteration without permission of installations which may cause danger, damage or nuisance. The
categories of installation which fall under this Act are
defined by amvb (general instrument of administration). This
amvb was enacted by a Royal Decree of 30/1/53, and covers almost
all enterprises of any size. In particular Article 1, Section
VIII mentions installations for the storage, processing or
destruction of waste. Generally speaking, under the Nuisance
Act, the local authority is the competent body.

Various provincial regulations relate to the problems of waste
processing and soil pollution. All provinces have regulations
controlling the landscape. In most cases, measures are imposed
which restrict the siting of tips for the deposit of rubble.
These prohibitions may be waived under licence or exemption.

The Law on Wastes (No. 455 of 23/6/77) establishes the policy
that each province is responsible for the wastes generated within
it. Thus, although national government is responsible for
formulating policy on wastes, implementation of this policy will
be the responsibility of the provincial governments. Policy
for the deposit of demolition and construction wastes has for
several years been that these wastes should be disposed of at
sites especially reserved for them. Whilst this is not as yet a
legal requirement, many municipalities have in fact implemented
this policy.

Although Law No. 455 came into effect in June 1977, it will
be some years before all of the policies envisaged during the
drafting of this Bill can be implemented. In particular, the
national authorities recognise that there is significant uncontrolled tipping of demolition and construction wastes at the
present time (the SVA has estimated 50% of this type of discharge
is uncontrolled). It is planned to prohibit this form of disposal
before 1982.

A.9.9   United Kingdom

The Control of Pollution Act 1974 is the only legal provision
specifically relating to the deposit on land of inert, non-toxic
industrial wastes such as construction and demolition wastes.
Part 1 of this Act deals with waste on land, and provides for
the implementation of many of the recommendations of the Working
Groups on the Disposal of Solid Toxic Waste and Refuse Disposal
(set up in 1964 and 1967 respectively). This Act provides the
statutory framework for a systematic and co-ordinated approach
to waste collection and disposal.

The Act provides that a waste disposal authority may take such
necessary steps for the purpose of reclaiming fractions of the
waste (Section 20), or utilise the waste for the generation of
heat or electricity (Section 21). It includes a requirement that
each authority should draw up a waste disposal plan, and in

doing so consider possibilities for recovering materials from waste (Section 2). This latter provision has only recently been implemented (1/7/78).

The Health and Safety at Work Act (1974) imposes a duty on employers to ensure, as far as is practicable, the health and safety at work of all of their employees. Section 2 (2) to 2(6) of this Act (implemented on 1/10/78), spell out the duties of the employer, provide for the publication of the employer's safety policy, and provide for the appointment of safety representatives by recognised trade unions.

There are several other Acts of Parliament which are applicable to certain aspects of demolition and construction work. These include:

-       Asbestos Regulations, 1969 SI No. 690

-       Clean Air Act, 1956

-       Deposit of Poisonous Wastes Act, 1972

-       Explosives Acts, 1875 and 1923

-       Factories Act, 1961.

Appendix 10. Summary of international research concerning demolition and the re-use of materials

A.10.1   The Three Countries Project

A.10.1.1   "Demolition, Re-use and Dismantling of Concrete"

Three sub-projects, entitled "New demolition techniques", "Re-use of demolished concrete", and "Demountable construction" are being undertaken in Germany, Belgium and the Netherlands. Various laboratories and institutions in each country are involved with the work, The secretariat is the Stichting Commissie voor Uitvoering Van Research (CUR) in the Netherlands. The work is largely financed by national authorities. An application to the Commission of the European Communities for a subsidy with regard to this research has been made. In Belgium and in the Netherlands, work began in 1977. In Germany, problems of finance have delayed the commencement of the work.

A.10.2   RILEM Committee

A.10.2.1   "Demolition and Re-use of concrete"

The committee is surveying existing methods of demolition, and studying relevant Codes of Safety and Regulations in various countries. It is further evaluating the possible savings, on a cost and energy basis, from the re-use of waste concrete in new construction. The committee has not as yet reported any results as work has only recently begun.

Appendix 11.   Summary of research concerning the demolition of concrete

A.11.1   Methods being evaluated by the Centre Scientifique et
                Technique de la Construction, Belgium (CSTC)

                Both of the two projects summarised below are being undertaken
                as part of the "Three Countries Project", see Appendix 10.

A.11.1.1   Explosives demolition

                The CSTC is currently experimenting with the use of explosives
                to fragment large reinforced concrete masses to a very fine
                mean particle size, leaving clean ferrous metal available for
                recyling. The work undertaken to date suggests that the total
                costs of this operation will be approximately BF 600/m^3 of
                concrete, from which about 50 kg of steel per cubic metre of
                concrete will be available for recovery. Based on current scrap
                prices the net cost of comminution of reinforced concrete
                structures using explosives is thus approximately BF 500/m^3
                (BF 210/tonne).

A.11.1.2   Demolition by pulverising plant

                The CSTC is also investigating the claims of a French manufacturer
                of pulverising plant. The "Concasseur Brocas" it is claimed will
                pulverise reinforced concrete structures at a rate of 25-30 tonnes
                per hour.

                The structure is situated on a grill, and is attacked by two
                hammers which rotate in opposing directions. Under the impact
                of the hammers, traction and shear forces are set up which result
                in fracture of the concrete mass. It is at this stage that the
                'Concasseur Brocas' differs from conventional crushing plant,
                which rely on compressive forces to fragment concrete.

                The concrete pieces are continually attacked by the hammers
                until they are small enough to pass through a calibration sieve.
                The steel reinforcing which remains is ejected from the grill
                surround through hydraulically operated lateral doors.

                Reinforced concrete samples, both specially prepared and normal
                structures arising from demolition have been sent to the manu-
                facturers of this plant for testing. The results of the tests
                are reported as excellent. The steel was completely separated,

whilst the concrete was reduced to fine particle size with good distribution (50% of the fragmented concrete had a particle size less than 15mm). Operating costs, amortising capital over five years, are quoted as BF 240 per cubic metre.

A.11.2   Studies at the University of Eindhoven, the Netherlands

The Materials Technology Laboratory of the Department of Architecture is evaluating the application of surface active agents to concrete in order to reduce the energy requirement for concrete pulverisation. Solutions are chosen for their molecular structure to reduce the strength of the molecular bonds at the surface of the concrete. If force is then applied to the concrete (e.g. crushing), fragmentation takes place more easily.

It is claimed that such techniques may reduce the energy requirement for fragmentation by a factor of 10, and certainly by factors of 2 or 3. Research is continuing in three main areas:

-       optimal choice of surface agent

-       design and materials specification for crusher blades

-       methods of application of surface agent.

If sufficient funds are made available, it is hoped to proceed to pilot plant testing by 1981-82.

A.11.3   The Cavitating Water Jet

Research and pilot studies in the USA have suggested that cavitating water jets may be an effective and economic method for concrete size reduction (1, 2).

At sufficiently high pressures water jets will cut most materials including concrete, stone and even steel. When cavitation bubbles are introduced in the nozzle of a water jet, the rate of cutting will vary according to the distance between the nozzle of the jet and the material. When impact occurs simultaneous with the collapse of the vapour bubbles, the intense compression waves radiating out from the point of implosion of the bubbles cause stresses in the material above its fatigue and even its ultimate stress limit. This is the basis of the cavitating water jet.

---

1.   Butler D.M., Graham W.M. 'Dismantling Railroad Freight Cars'. Booz Allen Applied Research Inc. for U.S. Department of Health, Education and Welfare, 1969.

2.   Carn A.F., Johnson V.E. 'Further Applications of the Cavitating Water Jet Method'. Hydronautics Inc. U.S.A., paper D2, Second International Symposium on Jet Cutting Technology, BHRA Fluid Engineering.

Appendix 12.   Contact list

<u>CONTACT LIST</u>

Main contacts made during the course of the study are listed
below by country.

<u>BELGIUM AND LUXEMBOURG</u>

Ministère de Santé Publique et de la Famille	Mr Renson	Brussels
Ministère Politique Scientifique et Technique	Mr Van Vaerenburg	Brussels
Ministère de Travaux Publique, Département d'Urbanism	Service demolition	Brussels
Ministère des Affaires Economiques	Direction des Mises	Brussels
Société Nationale de Logement		Brussels
Ministère de Santé Publique et de l'Environnement,	Mr Veverpole	Luxembourg
Institute Nationale de Statistique		Brussels
Centre Administratif		Liege
Société de Développement Régional pour la Wallonie	Mr J. Paligot	Namur
Centre national de documentation scientifique et technique		Brussels
STATEC (Luxembourg Statistical Office)	Mr Kirschmeyer	Luxembourg
Centre Scientifique et Technique de la Construction	Mr C. de Pauw Mr E. Rousseau	Brussels
Centre de Récherches Routières		Brussels
Office du Promotion Industrielle		Brussels

Confédération Nationale de la Construction		Brussels
Commission Belge du béton armé		Brussels
Groupement Nationale de l'industrie de la terre cuite		Brussels
Fédération de Travaux Publique		
Entreprises Canivet	Mr J. Canivet	Brussels
Entreprises Sogetra	Mr Gheur	Brussels
Entreprises De Nul		
Entreprises Froidecour		Brussels
Entreprises Socol		

DENMARK

Solid Wastes Division, Ministry of the Environment	Mr E. Moltke Mr A.S. Welinder	Copenhagen
Bolingministeriet (Ministry of Housing)	Mr Hjelme	Copenhagen
Grundejernes Sanerinesselskab	Mr B. Lundt	Copenhagen
Government Building Research Institute	Mr E. Brandt	Horsholm
Building and Construction Division, Technological Institute	Mr P. Christiansen Mr N. Thanlow	Tåstrup
Kunstakademiets Arkitektskole	Mr J. Englemark	Copenhagen
Danmarks Statistik		Copenhagen
Det Danske Stalvalsevaerk A/s	Mr U. Skjernov	Frederiksvaerk
Entreprenørforeningen	Mr N. Christiansen	Copenhagen
E. Struve Entreprenør Aps.	Mr E. Struve	Copenhagen
Børge Jakobsens Vognmandsforretning	Mr Laursen	Rødovre
Bates Ventil Saekke A/s	Mr R. Hansen Mr K. Christiansen	Copenhagen

FRANCE

Ministère de l'Environnement et de l'Equipement	Mme A. de Larderel	Paris
Ministère du Bâtiment et Travaux Publique		Paris
Centre Experimental de Récherches et d'Etudes du Bâtiment	Mr Landjerit	Paris
Service Economique de la Fédération de la Construction	Mr Schmidt	Paris
Laboratoire Central des Ponts et Chaussées	Mr L. Primel	Orly
Laboratoire des Ponts et Chaussées	Mr S. Maupui	Paris
Service des Espaces Vertes	Mr Bader	La Cour Neuve
Ville de le Havre	Mr Berne	Le Havre
Directeur adjoint du Service Technique	Mr Massabo Mr Bernet	Nice
Ville de Lyon	Mr Allarousse	Lyon
Réunion Internationale des Laboratoires d'Essais et de Récherches sur les Matériaux et les Constructions	Mme Genevieve	Paris Lyon
Centre Experimental de Récherches de l'industrie de Lients Hydraulique	Mr Venuat	Paris
Centre Scientifique et Technique du Bâtiment		Paris
Fédération des Entrepreneurs de Démolition		Paris
Entreprises Jean Lefebre	Mr Dig	Paris
Entreprises Gascheau	Mr Durant	Le Havre
Entreprises Pagan	Mr Pagan	Lyon
Entreprises Dussel	Mr P. Dussel	Paris
Entreprises Genier	Mr P. Genier	Paris
Entreprises Saussier	Mr G. Saussier	Argenteuil Paris

Etablissements Bruneau	Mr Boutard	Boulogne-sur-Seine
Entreprises Duprès	Mr Duprès	Paris/Creteil

FEDERAL REPUBLIC OF GERMANY

Umweltbundesamt	Prof. Goosmann	Berlin
Bundesanstalt für Geowissenschaft und Rohstoffe	Prof. Luttig	Hannover
Senat für Bau- und Wohnungs-wesen	Herr Blüme	Berlin
Siedlungsverband Ruhrkohlen-bezirk (SVR)	Herr Rimmasch	Essen
Deutscher Schrott Verband	Herr Landers	Düsseldorf
Deutscher Abbruch Verband		Düsseldorf
Forschungsinstitut der Zement-industrie	Herr Beck	Düsseldorf
Landers-Verfahrenstechnik	Herr Landers	Wesel
Firma Schilling KG	Herr Schilling	Hannover
Firma Schmids	Herr Siemoneit	Duisburg
Baustoffhandel Rothenburgsort		Hamburg
Firma Kneucker	Mr Armbruster	Mannheim
Firma Rosenhoff	Mr Denner	Dortmund
Hanzheim Co.	Mr Hanzheim	Cologne
Firma Liesegang	Mr Ockenfelz	Cologne
Firma Goertz	Mr Weyman	Duisburg

IRELAND

Building and Construction Division, Department of the Environment	Mr Licken	Dublin
Environmental Services, Department of the Environment	Mr Watson	Dublin

Ministry for Local Government	Mr Coffrey	Dublin
Dublin Corporation	Mr I. Keating	Dublin
Construction Division, National Institute for Physical Planning and Construction Research	Mr C. O'Rourke	Dublin
Construction Division, Institute for Industrial Research and Standards	Mr S.F. Dunleavy	Dublin
Project Identification Section, Industrial Development Authority	Mr T. O'Rourke	Dublin

ITALY

Ministry for Industry		Rome
Ministry of the Interior		Rome
Italian State Institute for Statistics		Rome
Ecology Assessor, Commune di Milano	Dott. Ferrario	Milan
Milan Public Cleansing Authority		Milan
Associazione Nazionale Costruttori Edili	Dott. Ing. Fossi	Rome
Associazione fra Imprese Edili a Complementari della Provincia di Milano	Sig. Porta	Milan
Centro Ricerche Economiche Sociologiche e di Mercato nella Edilizia	Dott. Sossetti	Rome
Socogen S.p.a.	Geom. Ronchetti	Milan
Asti & Grignani S.p.a.		Milan
Caem S.a.s.		Milan

THE NETHERLANDS

Ministry of the Environment and Public Health	Dr Erasmus Mr Van Wijk Mr Van de Schaaf Mr Smit	Den Haag

Association of Netherlands Municipalities		Den Haag
R.O.T.E.B., Municipality of Rotterdam	Mr Hoogland Mr Gordon	Rotterdam
Housing Department, Municipality of Den Haag	Mr Spee Mr Schrader	Den Haag
Stichting Verwijdering	Mr Kreiter Mr van Vliet Mr Teeuwen	Amersfoort
Department of Building Materials and Building Construction, T.N.O.	Ir. Wiebemga	Rijswijk
Stichting Commissie voor Uitvoering van Research	Mr Van Riel, Director	Zoetermeer
Rijkswegenbouwlaboratorium	Mr Hendricks	
Bouwcentrum	Ir. Volbeda, Director	Rotterdam
Centraal Bureau voor de Statistiek		Den Haag
Economic Institute for Building Activities		Den Haag
University of Technology	Professor Kreijger	Eindhoven
University of Delft	Professor Wittman, Prof. of Materials	Delft
European Demolition Association	Mr Basart, Secretary General	Den Haag
B.A.B.E.X. - Association of Netherlands Demolition Contractors		Den Haag
L. Korting B.V.	Mr L. Korting	Amsterdam
Aannemingsbedrijf Van Eck C.V.	Mr H. Van Eck	Den Haag
Economic Department, Royal Netherlands Embassy	Miss Van Wyngaarden	London

UNITED KINGDOM

Department of the Environment	Mr B. Gulley Miss Wilcox Mr Strong Mr Swift	London
Public Health Department, Greater London Council	Mr Millard	London

Public Health Engineering Department G.L.C. Scientific Branch		London
Planning Department, Lambeth Council	Mr Kibby	London
Berkshire County Council	Mr King	Reading
West Sussex County Council		Chichester
East Sussex County Council		Lewes
Stafford County Council	Mr P. Taylor	Staff
Building Research Establishment	Dr Everett Dr Nixon Mr Musannif	Watford
Transport and Road Research Laboratory	Mr Sherwood	Crowthorne
Construction Industry Research and Information Association	Mr Nicholson	London
National Federation of Building Trades Employers	Mr J. Huxtable	London
Sheerness Steel	Mr James, Director	Sheerness
Timber Research and Development Association	Dr O.P. Hanson	High Wycombe
British Reclamation Industries Confederation	Mr Bainbridge	Huntingdon
Brick Development Association Ltd	Mr K. Thomas	Windsor
Cement and Concrete Association		London
British Secondary Metals Association		London
National Building Agency		London
Organisation of European Aluminium Smelters		London
Aluminium Federation Limited		London
Princes Risborough Laboratory, Building Research Establishment		Aylesbury
National Federation of Demolition Contractors	Mr R. Elford, General Secretary	London
Charles Griffiths Ltd	Mr P. Griffiths, MD Mr Moyes, Director	Barking
London Demolition Co. Ltd	Mr T. Greenham, MD	London

Norman Hill (Twickenham) Ltd	Mr Hill, MD	Isleworth
Charles Brand (Dundee) Ltd	Mr W. Brand, MD and President, NFCD	Dundee
S.A.M. Contractors	Mr Swinnerton, MD	Willenhall
Wilment Brothers Ltd	Mr Walker, Director	London

References

1.   Abfallbeseitigungsgesetz 1972.

2.   Private Communication; Municipality of The Hague.

3.   Rijkswegenbouwlaboratorium, Netherlands.

4.   Use of waste materials and by-products in road construction
      OECD, 1977.

5.   Norman Hill Ltd., Isleworth, U.K.

6.   Quad City Solid Wastes project - an interim report.
      U.S. Department of Health, Education and Welfare, 1967.

7.   Gesetz über Umweltstatistiken, 1974.

8.   Basic Sources: - Ministry of Housing
                      - Grundejernes Saneringsselskab s.m.b.a.

9.   Bouw - en Sloopafval, Interim rapport SVA/1759, September 1976.

10.   Building Research Establishment, Unpublished study.

11.   Source: Italian State Institute for Statistics, (ISTAT).

12.   Source: Der Senator für Bau- und Wohnungswesen, December 1978.

13.   Nixon P.J. "The use of materials from demolition in construction".
      Resources Policy, December 1976.

14.   "De vaste industriële afvalstoffen in Limburg, Oost - Vlaanderen,
      West-Vlaanderen, Vlaams Brabout en de agglomeratie Brussel -
      Hoofdstad". S.C.K./C.E.N. 1974.

15.   "Les déchets du bois". Courrier de l'industriel du Bois et de
      l'Ameublement. Centre Technique du Bois 1/78.

16.   Primel L., Tourenq C. "Les granulats de remplacement".
      Annales des Mines, 12, 167-178, 1976.

17.   "Les déchets solides – propositions pour une politique". Rapport
        du groupe d'études sur l'élimination des résidus solides.
        Documentation Française, Paris 1974.

18.   Source: Service d'études de marché sur construction, 1977.

19.   Basic sources: – Annual Bulletin of Construction Statistics,
                           Ministry of Public Works

                         – Housing and Construction Statistics, D.O.E.

20.   Basic source: Annual Bulletin of Housing and Building Statistics
                        for Europe, 1963, 1969, 1976.

21.   "Europe", 9/9/76.

22.   Quarterly Bulletin of Industrial Production – Eurostat, 1978.

23.   "Resources in America's Future", U.S. Aluminium Association,
        John Hopkins, U.S.A. 1969.

24.   Metal Statistics, 42nd and 64th Editions, Metallgesellschaft,
        Frankfurt.

25.   Basic data – Aluminium Industry Council.

26.   Aluminium Federation Limited.

27.   Personal communication; S. Landers of Landers Firmengruppe.

28.   Resource Recovery Market in Western Europe, published by Frost
        and Sullivan, March 1977.

29.   "Aggregates by Rail", Modern Railways, August 1978.

30.   Stamatia Frondistou – Yannas and Taichi Itoh, "Economic
        Feasibility of Concrete Recycling". J. Structural Division ASCI.
        April 1977, pp 885-899.

31.   Frondistou-Yannas, "Waste Concrete as Aggregate for New Concrete",
        ACI Journal August 1977 pp 373-378.

32.   See Economics of Recyling. (Part A, Section 8). Report prepared
        by Environmental Resources Limited for the Commission of the
        European Communities, published by Graham and Trotman 1978.

33.   Basic source: World Cement Market in Figures.

34.   Department of Engineering, Technical College of Nova Scotia,
        Canada.

35.   Alfred Process Plant, Oakwood Chemical Works, Sandy Lane,
        Worksop, Nottinghamshire.

36.   World Commodity Outlook 1978/79 – Industrial Raw Materials –
        published by the Economist Intelligence Unit, October 1978.

37.   Boligen 1970, Statistical year book (Danmarks Statistik).

38.   Abfallwirtschaftsprogramm, 1975.

39.   Overzicht afvalverwijdering in Nederland. SVA/2430/175,
           December 1977.

40.   Bouw - en Sloopafval. CBS 7/12/77.

41   Puinafvoerplan Zuid-Holland. Provinciale Staten van Zuid-Holland,
           10/6/77.

42.   Wilson D.G., Weisman R.M. "An Investigation of the Potential
           for Resource Recovery from Demolition Wastes". M.I.T., October
           1976.

43.   Kinnersly P., "Asbestos: unsafe at any concentration". New
           Civil Engineering No. 195 20th May 1976, pp 32 - 34.

44.   "Asbestos and alternative materials", The Architects Journal
           1/12/76 pp 1041 - 1050.

45.   Roskhill Report on Metals and Minerals : Asbestos. Second
           Edition 1976 and Statistical Supplement 1978. Roskhill Infor-
           mation Services Ltd.

46.   Kinnersly, P. "Asbestos: what can you do for safety?", New Civil
           Engineer No. 195, 27th May. 1976, pp 22-23.

47.   "Asbestos-based Materials for the Building and Shipbuilding
           Industries and Electrical and Engineering Insulation". The
           Asbestos Research Council, Control and Safety Guide No. 5, 1977.

48.   Protective Equipment in the Asbestos Industry (Respiratory
           Equipment and Protective Clothing). Asbestos Research Council,
           Control and Safety Guide No. 1, 1978.

49.   The Asbestos Regulations 1969 - SI 690, HMSO, 1969.

50.   Personal Communication, Asbestos International Association,
           London, March 1979.